PRAYERS OF THE MIDNIGHT WARRIORS

"A Midnight Warfare Handbook to Overcome Powers of Darkness and Disrupt Their Activities"

TIMOTHY ATUNNISE

Glovim Publishing House
Atlanta, Georgia

PRAYERS OF THE MIDNIGHT WARRIORS

Glovim Publishing House
1078 Citizens Pkwy
Suite A
Morrow, Georgia 30260

glovimbooks@gmail.com
www.glovimonline.org

Printed in the United States of America

Table of Contents

Introduction

Awakening the Midnight Warriors

In the heart of the night, when the world is cloaked in shadow and most souls slumber in the tranquility of dreams, there exists a chosen few. They are the Midnight Warriors, an army of believers who rise when darkness threatens to devour the light. These warriors are not ordinary; they are equipped with a divine arsenal, armed with faith, and fueled by a fervent connection to the Creator of all.

The battle they wage is not fought on earthly battlegrounds but in the spiritual realm, where the powers of darkness seek to undermine, oppress, and destroy. It is a realm unseen by the naked eye, yet its influence extends into every facet of our lives. It is the battleground of the soul, where the destiny of nations and individuals alike hangs in the balance. It is in this spiritual darkness that the Midnight Warriors find their calling.

Prayers of the Midnight Warriors: A Midnight Warfare Handbook to Overcome Powers of Darkness and Disrupt Their Activities is a sacred guide for those who have heard the call of midnight, who have felt the urgency to rise above the mundane and engage in a battle that transcends time and space. This handbook is not for the faint of heart, for the journey it undertakes is not for the lukewarm or the half-hearted. It is a clarion call to the spiritually awakened, those who understand that our world is a battleground where light and darkness collide.

In these pages, you will discover the ancient art of midnight warfare, a practice deeply rooted in the Christian faith. It is a tradition as old as time itself, passed down through generations of faithful believers who understood the significance of the midnight hour. It was at midnight that the Israelites were delivered from the bondage of Egypt, and it was at midnight that Paul and Silas sang hymns of praise in their prison cell, shaking the very foundations of their captivity.

The Midnight Warriors are not bound by time zones or physical locations. They are united by a shared understanding that the midnight hour is a sacred and potent time for spiritual warfare. It is a time when the veil between the natural and supernatural is thin, allowing believers to access realms of divine power and authority that are often hidden during the day.

This handbook is a comprehensive guide to midnight warfare, filled with prayers, decrees, and declarations that will empower you to overcome the powers of darkness and disrupt their nefarious activities. It is a treasure trove of spiritual insights and practical strategies that have been tested and proven in the heat of battle. It is a roadmap for your journey from spiritual passivity to divine assertiveness.

As you delve into the chapters of this handbook, you will learn how to put on the full armor of God, how to plead the blood of Jesus for protection, and how to wield the sword of the Spirit with precision. You will discover the secrets of fasting and prayer, the power of worship in the midnight hour, and the authority you possess as a child of the Most High. You will be equipped to confront the principalities and powers that seek to hinder your progress and oppress your life.

But this book is not just a manual for warfare; it is also a source of inspiration and encouragement. Within these pages, you will find stories of ordinary people who, when faced with extraordinary challenges, rose to become Midnight Warriors. Their testimonies serve as beacons of hope, reminding us that no matter how fierce the battle, victory is assured for those who stand in faith.

As you embark on this journey, remember that you are not alone. You are part of a global community of Midnight Warriors, connected by a common purpose and a shared faith. Together, we will rise in the midnight hour, our voices raised in prayer and worship, our hearts aflame with the fire of the Holy Spirit. Together, we will overcome the powers of darkness and disrupt their activities, for we serve a God who is mighty to save and faithful to His promises.

Prepare yourself, dear reader, for the adventure of a lifetime. The midnight hour is calling, and the battle is about to begin. Are you ready to join the ranks of the Midnight Warriors and take your place in the divine symphony of spiritual warfare? The journey awaits, and the victory is assured for those who dare to answer the call.

In the pages that follow, you will find the tools, the knowledge, and the inspiration you need to become a formidable force in the realm of midnight warfare. Let the journey begin.

Chapter 1

Unleash the Midnight Warriors:
A Call to Battle

In the quiet of the midnight hour, when the world slumbers and the stars paint a canvas of darkness, there exists a realm often unnoticed by many—a realm where spiritual warfare takes center stage. It is a battleground where the forces of light and darkness clash, where destiny is shaped, and where the power of prayer rises like a mighty warrior. Welcome to the realm of the Midnight Warriors, where the call to battle echoes through the corridors of heaven.

The Midnight Hour: A Divine Appointment

To understand the significance of the midnight hour in spiritual warfare, we must first recognize its importance in the biblical narrative. Throughout the Bible, the midnight hour is a time when God chooses to reveal His glory, execute His judgments, and deliver His people from the hands of their enemies.

One of the most profound instances of the midnight hour in the Bible is found in the book of Exodus. The Israelites, enslaved in Egypt, cried out for deliverance, and God heard their cries. He appointed a specific time, the midnight hour, to execute His judgment upon the oppressors and lead His people to freedom. It was at midnight that the Angel of Death passed through Egypt, sparing the homes marked with the blood of the Passover lamb.

The Midnight Watchmen

In the depths of the night, when darkness seeks to engulf our souls, God calls forth His Midnight Warriors—those who are vigilant, discerning, and unyielding in their pursuit of His will. These spiritual watchmen, often referred to as intercessors, stand on the front lines of the spiritual battlefield. They are the ones who heed the call to battle when others are fast asleep.

The Midnight Warriors are not bound by the constraints of time or sleep. They are men and women who understand the gravity of the spiritual battles that rage around them. They recognize that the midnight hour is a divine appointment with destiny, a time when they can access the supernatural power of God to confront and overcome the forces of darkness.

The Armor of God Unveiled

To engage in spiritual warfare as a Midnight Warrior, one must be equipped with the full armor of God. The apostle Paul, in his letter to the

Ephesians, provides a detailed description of this spiritual armor. Each piece serves a unique purpose in the battle against the powers of darkness.

1. The Belt of Truth: Truth is the foundation of our spiritual armor. In a world filled with deception and lies, we must gird ourselves with the unshakable truth of God's Word.

2. The Breastplate of Righteousness: Righteousness protects our hearts from the enemy's attacks. It is the assurance of our standing before God as forgiven and redeemed.

3. The Shoes of Peace: Our readiness to share the Gospel of peace with others is our firm footing in the midst of chaos and conflict.

4. The Shield of Faith: Faith is our defense against the fiery darts of the enemy. It is the unwavering belief in God's promises.

5. The Helmet of Salvation: Salvation secures our minds against doubt and despair. It assures us of our eternal destiny in Christ.

6. The Sword of the Spirit: The Word of God is our offensive weapon. It is the sharp, two-edged sword that pierces through darkness and sets the captives free.

As Midnight Warriors, we must put on this armor daily, not just when the battle rages, but in the quiet moments of preparation during the midnight watch. It is this spiritual armor that empowers us to stand firm in the face of adversity and to advance the kingdom of God in the darkest of times.

Prayer: The Weapon of Warfare

At the heart of the Midnight Warrior's arsenal lies the weapon of prayer. Prayer is not a passive activity; it is a violent and transformative force that shakes the very foundations of the spiritual realm. It is a direct line of communication with the Creator of the universe, and it is our greatest privilege and responsibility as believers.

Midnight prayers are unique in their intensity and focus. They are prayers that pierce through the silence of the night and ascend to the throne of God with a sense of urgency. These prayers are not whispered timidly but declared boldly, for we know that the enemy trembles at the name of Jesus.

In the midnight hour, we unleash the power of prayer to disrupt the activities of the powers of darkness. We declare the Word of God with authority, knowing that every decree aligns with heaven's agenda. As the psalmist David declared, "At midnight I rise to give you thanks for your righteous laws" (Psalm 119:62, NIV). Midnight is a time of thanksgiving, praise, and warfare, all rolled into one.

The Call to Battle

Midnight Warriors, the call to battle is upon us. The darkness may be deep, but the light within us is greater. We are not passive observers of the spiritual realm; we are active participants in the divine drama unfolding in the midnight hour. The battles we face may be fierce, but the victory is assured through our Lord and Savior, Jesus Christ.

In the chapters that follow, we will delve deeper into the strategies and decrees of Midnight Warfare. We will explore the role of fasting, the power of worship, the authority of the believer, and the miraculous interventions that await those who dare to stand as Midnight Warriors.

As you embark on this journey, remember that you are not alone. Countless warriors around the world join you in the midnight watch. Together, we will disrupt the activities of darkness, advance the kingdom of God, and usher in a new dawn of spiritual victory. The call to battle is now. Will you answer?

Warfare Prayer

1. In the name of Jesus, I declare that the midnight hour is a divine appointment with destiny, and I will not miss it.

2. By the blood of the Lamb, I decree that the forces of darkness have no power over me in the midnight hour.

3. I put on the full armor of God, and I declare that I am a well-equipped Midnight Warrior.

4. In Jesus' name, I fasten the Belt of Truth around my waist, declaring that I am rooted in the unshakable truth of God's Word.

5. I declare that the Breastplate of Righteousness shields my heart from the attacks of the enemy.

6. With the Shoes of Peace, I step forward confidently, ready to share the Gospel of peace in the darkest of times.

7. I raise the Shield of Faith, extinguishing every fiery dart of doubt and fear that the enemy sends my way.

8. In Jesus' name, I secure the Helmet of Salvation, guarding my mind against deception and despair.

9. I wield the Sword of the Spirit, which is the Word of God, as a mighty weapon against the powers of darkness.

10. By the authority of Jesus' name, I declare that I am a vigilant Midnight Warrior, standing watch in the night.

11. I proclaim that I am not bound by the constraints of time or sleep, but I am alert and discerning in the midnight hour.

12. In the name of Jesus, I rise as a spiritual watchman, ready to engage in battle when others are asleep.

13. I decree that the midnight hour is a time of divine revelation and supernatural encounters with God.

14. By the blood of Jesus, I mark my household as a place of divine protection in the midnight hour.

15. I release the power of praise and worship as a weapon of warfare in the midnight watch.

16. I declare that my midnight prayers pierce through the silence of the night and reach the throne of God with urgency.

17. In Jesus' name, I disrupt the activities of the powers of darkness with the authority given to me as a believer.

18. I decree that my prayers are not timid whispers but bold declarations of God's promises and truth.

19. By the blood of Jesus, I plead for the deliverance of those in bondage to darkness.

20. I declare that I am a vessel of God's light, dispelling the spiritual darkness in my sphere of influence.

21. I take authority over every demonic stronghold that seeks to hinder God's purposes in my life.

22. In the name of Jesus, I rebuke every spirit of deception and confusion, and I release a spirit of discernment.

23. I declare that I am an overcomer by the blood of the Lamb and the word of my testimony.

24. I release the angels of God to encamp around me and protect me in the midnight hour.

25. By the authority of Jesus' name, I break every chain and shackle that binds me or my loved ones.

26. I proclaim that I am a vessel of healing, and I release the healing power of God in the midnight hour.

27. I declare that supernatural dreams and visions are my portion, revealing God's plans and strategies.

28. In Jesus' name, I rise above fear and anxiety, for the Spirit of power, love, and a sound mind dwells within me.

29. I decree that my prayers release signs and wonders that testify to the glory of God.

30. I take authority over every principality and power that opposes God's kingdom in my life and in the nations.

31. By the blood of Jesus, I stand in the midnight courts, presenting my petitions before the throne of grace.

32. I declare that I am a midnight worshipper, offering songs of victory and adoration to my King.

33. In the name of Jesus, I release supernatural wisdom and understanding for the challenges I face.

34. I bind the spirits of darkness and loose the presence of God in every situation.

35. I declare that the enemy's plans are exposed, and his schemes are thwarted by the light of God's truth.

36. By the authority of Jesus' name, I release a fresh outpouring of the Holy Spirit in my life.

37. I declare that I am a vessel of love, and I extend love and forgiveness to those who have wronged me.

38. In Jesus' name, I celebrate my victories in the midnight battles, knowing that the battle belongs to the Lord.

39. I decree that the legacy of Midnight Warriors will be passed down from generation to generation.

40. I declare that as a Midnight Warrior, I am more than a conqueror through Him who loves me, and I will see the victory of the Lord in every area of my life.

Chapter 2

Storming the Gates of the Night:
Strategies for Victory

In the darkest hours of the night, when the world sleeps and shadows loom large, the midnight warrior arises. This chapter is your training ground, your spiritual boot camp, where we delve into the profound strategies that will lead you to victory in the battlefield of the spirit. It's time to storm the gates of the night, armed with knowledge, faith, and divine authority.

The Midnight Hour and Its Significance

Before we dive into the strategies, let's understand the significance of the midnight hour in the realm of spiritual warfare. Midnight is a time when the supernatural intersects with the natural. It's a moment when the spiritual veil is thin, and the powers of darkness are most active. In the Bible, we see several instances where midnight played a pivotal role. The midnight hour was when Paul and Silas prayed and praised God in prison, leading to their miraculous deliverance (Acts 16:25-26).

The Gates of the Night: Identifying the Strongholds

To effectively storm the gates of the night, we must first identify the strongholds that the enemy has established in the darkness. These strongholds can take various forms: generational curses, addictions, fear, sickness, or even oppression. Identifying these strongholds is crucial because it enables us to target our prayers and decrees effectively.

The Power of Spiritual Mapping

Spiritual mapping is a strategic tool in midnight warfare. It involves researching and understanding the spiritual landscape of your region. Just as military commanders study the terrain before a battle, we must understand the spiritual terrain of our surroundings. This includes identifying areas with high crime rates, occult practices, or other signs of spiritual darkness.

Strategic Prayer Walks

Once you have a clear spiritual map, it's time to take action. Engage in strategic prayer walks. These are not ordinary strolls; they are intentional spiritual journeys. As you walk the streets of your neighborhood or city, you are declaring the authority of Christ and His light over every area. Pray against the strongholds you've identified and release God's power to break them.

Decrees of Authority

In the realm of midnight warfare, decrees are potent weapons. Decrees are authoritative statements based on God's Word. When you declare God's promises and truths, you are releasing His power into the situation. For example, you can declare, "By the blood of Jesus, I break every generational curse over my family," or "I decree health and healing in the name of Jesus." These decrees carry divine authority and can shatter the enemy's schemes.

The Weapon of Worship

Worship is a mighty weapon in the midnight hour. Just as Paul and Silas praised God in the prison cell, our worship can create seismic shifts in the spiritual realm. Worship invites the presence of God, and in His presence, darkness flees. Sing songs of victory, play instruments, and let the praises of God fill the atmosphere. As you worship, you're not just singing; you're waging war.

Fasting for Breakthrough

Fasting is another powerful strategy in midnight warfare. Fasting demonstrates our desperation for God's intervention. It weakens the flesh and strengthens the spirit. During your fast, pray fervently, seeking God's guidance and deliverance. Fasting can break the chains of bondage and open doors to supernatural breakthroughs.

The Company of Midnight Warriors

You are not alone in this battle. Seek out fellow midnight warriors who share your passion for spiritual warfare. Pray together, share insights, and encourage one another. The synergy of united prayers is formidable, and it amplifies your impact in the spiritual realm.

Becoming a Watchman

As a midnight warrior, you are called to be a watchman on the wall. This means being vigilant and discerning. Watch for signs of spiritual activity in your environment. Be discerning about dreams and visions, as they can often carry messages from the spiritual realm. Stay alert and responsive to the leading of the Holy Spirit.

The Midnight Triumph

Storming the gates of the night requires a combination of knowledge, faith, and strategic action. Armed with these strategies, you can be a formidable force in the realm of spiritual warfare. Remember, the midnight hour is not a time to fear but a time to rise in authority and take back what the enemy has stolen. The gates of the night will yield to the power of God working through you.

As you continue your journey as a midnight warrior, the victories you experience will not only transform your life but also impact your community and beyond. Stay bold, stay vigilant, and never underestimate the power of a warrior who storms the gates of the night with faith and authority.

Warfare Prayer

1. In the name of Jesus, I declare that I am a midnight warrior, called and equipped for victory!

2. By the blood of Jesus, I break every generational curse that has plagued my family's lineage.

3. I decree and declare that the gates of the night will not prevail against the light of Christ in me.

4. In Jesus' name, I bind and cast out every spirit of fear that has tormented my mind.

5. I release the power of the Holy Spirit to strengthen me for the battles of the night.

6. I declare that my prayers are strategic and effective, targeting the strongholds of darkness.

7. By the authority of Jesus, I take dominion over every area identified on my spiritual map.

8. I decree that the light of God's truth will expose and shatter every hidden scheme of the enemy.

9. In the name of Jesus, I declare that I am a watchman on the wall, discerning the signs of the times.

10. I bind and rebuke all demonic forces that seek to disrupt my prayer walks and spiritual journeys.

11. I release the fire of God's presence to consume every spiritual darkness in my region.

12. By the blood of Jesus, I break every addiction and stronghold that has held me captive.

13. I decree divine healing and restoration over my body, soul, and spirit.

14. In Jesus' name, I declare that I am more than a conqueror through Christ who strengthens me.

15. I release the power of worship to usher in God's glory and drive out every evil presence.

16. I decree that my worship is a weapon of mass destruction against the enemy's plans.

17. By the authority of Jesus, I silence every accusing voice and condemnation in my life.

18. I declare that my fasting is a spiritual catalyst, opening doors to supernatural breakthroughs.

19. I release angels to encamp around me, protecting me from all harm and danger.

20. In the name of Jesus, I decree that my dreams and visions are filled with divine revelation.

21. I bind and cast out all spirits of confusion and deception from my thoughts and dreams.

22. I decree that my prayers for my family and nation are powerful and effective.

23. By the blood of Jesus, I break the chains of poverty and lack in my life.

24. I release the abundance of God's provision and blessings over my finances.

25. In Jesus' name, I declare that I am a mighty intercessor, standing in the gap for others.

26. I bind and dismantle every stronghold of addiction and bondage in my community.

27. I release the peace of God to calm the storms in the lives of those around me.

28. By the authority of Jesus, I declare that the gates of opportunity will swing open for me.

29. I decree divine wisdom and understanding to navigate every situation in my life.

30. I release the power of unity among fellow midnight warriors, strengthening our impact.

31. In the name of Jesus, I declare that I am a victor, not a victim, in every circumstance.

32. I bind and rebuke all sickness and disease that dare to touch my body.

33. I release the healing virtue of Jesus to flow through every part of my being.

34. By the blood of Jesus, I break every yoke of oppression and depression in my life.

35. I decree that the joy of the Lord is my strength, and it drives away all sorrow.

36. In Jesus' name, I declare that I am a child of God, covered by His love and grace.

37. I bind and cast out all forces of darkness that oppose my destiny.

38. I release the favor of God to open doors of divine opportunities in my life.

39. By the authority of Jesus, I declare that I am an overcomer, and no weapon formed against me shall prosper.

40. I decree and declare that my midnight triumphs will resound to the glory of God and the defeat of the enemy.

Chapter 3

Arise, O Warrior!
The Armor of God Unveiled

In the darkest hours of the night, when the world sleeps and the veil between the natural and supernatural realms grows thin, the call to arms resounds through the spiritual realm. It is a summons for the midnight warriors, those bold and fearless believers who are willing to take their stand against the powers of darkness. In this chapter, we delve deep into the heart of spiritual warfare, unveiling the extraordinary power of God that equips and empowers these warriors.

The Midnight Awakening

The midnight hour is a sacred time for the warrior of God. It's a time when the world is still, but the spiritual battlefield is alive with activity. It's the time when God's chosen ones rise from their slumber, not in weariness but in anticipation of divine encounters. As the world sleeps, these warriors are wide awake, ready to engage in the supernatural.

The Midnight Connection: The concept of midnight holds a profound significance in the Bible. It's a time of divine visitations and breakthroughs. Think of Paul and Silas in the prison (Acts 16:25), or Jacob wrestling with the angel (Genesis 32:24-30). Midnight is when God often chooses to reveal His power and deliver His people.

The Armor of God

Before any warrior steps onto the battlefield, they must be properly equipped. In the realm of spiritual warfare, the armor of God is our divine attire. Each piece of this heavenly armor serves a specific purpose, and together, they form an impenetrable shield against the enemy's attacks.

The Belt of Truth: It is the foundation of our spiritual armor. It holds everything together and keeps us grounded in God's truth. In a world filled with deception, the belt of truth keeps us from stumbling.

The Breastplate of Righteousness: This vital piece protects our hearts, for out of the heart flows the issues of life (Proverbs 4:23). With righteousness as our breastplate, we are assured of God's favor and protection.

The Shoes of the Gospel of Peace: Our feet are shod with readiness to spread the message of peace and salvation. We march forward with the Good News, leaving no place for darkness to hide.

The Shield of Faith: Faith is our defense against the enemy's fiery darts of doubt and fear. With unwavering faith, we can extinguish every attack that comes our way.

The Helmet of Salvation: Our minds are guarded by the assurance of salvation. We have the mind of Christ (1 Corinthians 2:16), and this helmet protects us from the enemy's attempts to infiltrate our thoughts.

The Sword of the Spirit: This is our offensive weapon, the Word of God. It is a double-edged sword that can cut through any stronghold and bring down the enemy's defenses.

The Power Within

As midnight warriors, we are not mere mortals engaged in this battle; we are vessels of the Holy Spirit, carrying within us the same power that raised Jesus from the dead (Romans 8:11). This power is not dormant but is meant to be activated and unleashed in the midnight hour.

The Anointing: The anointing of the Holy Spirit empowers us for supernatural exploits. It's the divine oil that makes us effective in our mission. As we rise in prayer and worship at midnight, the anointing flows, breaking every yoke of bondage.

The Gifts of the Spirit: The Spirit equips us with spiritual gifts that are essential for warfare. The gift of discernment helps us identify the enemy's tactics, while the gift of prophecy releases words of edification, exhortation, and comfort to strengthen the body of Christ.

The Authority in Jesus' Name: At the mention of the name of Jesus, every knee must bow, in heaven and on earth (Philippians 2:10). Midnight warriors understand the authority they possess in the name of Jesus and use it to bind and rebuke the forces of darkness.

The Fire of Prayer: Midnight prayer is not a mere ritual; it is a fiery communion with God. It's where the supernatural and the natural converge. The fervent, effectual prayers of a righteous person avail much (James 5:16). In the midnight hour, our prayers become potent weapons of warfare.

The Battle Cry

Every warrior has a battle cry that rallies their fellow soldiers and strikes fear into the hearts of the enemy. In spiritual warfare, our battle cry is the Word of God itself. It is the proclamation of God's promises, the declaration of His victory, and the assertion of our authority.

The Decrees of Victory: As midnight warriors, we don't just pray; we decree and declare. We speak God's Word with unwavering faith, knowing that His Word does not return void but accomplishes its purpose (Isaiah 55:11).

The Sound of Worship: Worship is our battle cry. When we lift our voices in adoration and praise, the enemy is confounded. Remember the story of Jehoshaphat (2 Chronicles 20) when the armies of Israel were saved through worship. Midnight warriors understand the power of worship in warfare.

Embrace Your Calling

We've unveiled the extraordinary power of God that equips the midnight warrior. It's a power that transcends human understanding, a power that can move mountains and tear down strongholds. As you embrace your calling as a midnight warrior, remember that you are not alone. You are part of a vast army of believers who rise in the midnight hour to engage in spiritual warfare.

Arise, O warrior! Put on the full armor of God. Let the power of God within you be unleashed. Raise your battle cry with the Word of God and the sound of worship. The powers of darkness may tremble, but you, as a midnight warrior, are destined for victory. In the following chapters, we will delve even deeper into the strategies and tactics of midnight warfare, equipping you to disrupt the activities of the enemy and walk in the fullness of your calling.

Warfare Prayer

1. In the name of Jesus, I declare that I am a midnight warrior, called and equipped for spiritual warfare.

2. I put on the belt of truth, and I declare that I walk in God's divine truth and wisdom.

3. My heart is protected by the breastplate of righteousness. I declare that I am the righteousness of God in Christ Jesus.

4. With the shoes of the gospel of peace, I declare that I carry the message of peace and salvation wherever I go.

5. I raise the shield of faith, and I declare that no fiery dart of the enemy can penetrate my faith fortress.

6. I wear the helmet of salvation, and I declare that my mind is guarded by the assurance of God's saving grace.

7. I wield the sword of the Spirit, which is the Word of God. I declare that every word I speak in alignment with His Word is a mighty weapon.

8. In the authority of Jesus' name, I am anointed for breakthrough and spiritual victories.

9. I operate in the gifts of the Spirit. I declare discernment to recognize the enemy's tactics and the gift of prophecy to edify and exhort others.

10. In the name of Jesus, I rebuke and bind every demonic force that opposes God's purposes in my life and in the lives of others.

11. I release the fire of prayer in the midnight hour, knowing that my prayers are powerful and effective.

12. I decree and declare that God's promises in His Word are yes and amen in my life.

13. I raise my voice in worship and praise, knowing that the enemy trembles at the sound of my worship.

14. I declare that I am more than a conqueror through Christ who strengthens me.

15. In the name of Jesus, I break every chain and stronghold that has held me captive.

16. I declare that I walk in divine favor and protection because I am a child of the Most High God.

17. I take authority over every spirit of fear, doubt, and unbelief in Jesus' name.

18. I release the angels of God to encamp around me and protect me from all harm.

19. I declare that I am a vessel of honor, sanctified and set apart for God's purposes.

20. I speak life and blessings over my family, my community, and my nation.

21. I declare that I have the mind of Christ, and I reject every thought that is contrary to His truth.

22. I rebuke sickness and infirmity in my body, and I declare divine healing and health.

23. I break every generational curse and declare freedom and restoration over my bloodline.

24. In the name of Jesus, I bind and cast out every spirit of darkness that has hindered my progress.

25. I declare that I am a carrier of God's glory and His presence goes with me wherever I go.

26. I release the power of forgiveness and let go of any bitterness or resentment in my heart.

27. I declare that my prayers at midnight are a sweet aroma to God, and He hears and answers them.

28. In the authority of Jesus' name, I release divine wisdom and revelation for every situation I face.

29. I take authority over every storm in my life and declare peace and calm in Jesus' name.

30. I declare that I am a light in the darkness, and I shine brightly for the glory of God.

31. I speak blessings and prosperity into every area of my life, knowing that God delights in my prosperity.

32. I break every curse of poverty and lack, and I declare abundance and provision.

33. In the name of Jesus, I silence every accusation and condemnation of the enemy.

34. I declare that I am an overcomer, and no weapon formed against me shall prosper.

35. I release the power of the blood of Jesus to cleanse and purify every area of my life.

36. I take authority over the spiritual atmosphere in my home and declare it a place of peace and worship.

37. I declare that I am a vessel of revival, and God's revival fire burns within me.

38. I speak blessings and favor over my enemies, knowing that love and kindness conquer all.

39. In the name of Jesus, I break every curse of witchcraft and sorcery that has been sent against me.

40. I declare that I am a victorious warrior, and I will see the goodness of the Lord in the land of the living.

Chapter 4

Pleading the Blood:
Your Weapon of Divine Protection

In the battlefield of spiritual warfare, there exists a potent weapon, a shield of invincibility that has been entrusted to the faithful warriors of the midnight hour. This weapon is none other than the precious and powerful Blood of Jesus Christ. In this chapter, we will delve into the depths of this divine protection, understanding its significance, and learning how to wield it with unwavering faith and authority.

The Crimson Thread of Redemption

To truly grasp the magnitude of "pleading the blood," we must first journey back to the very foundation of our faith. It is a crimson thread that weaves its way through the tapestry of human history, from the Garden of Eden to the hill of Calvary. This thread symbolizes the redemptive work of Jesus Christ, who willingly shed His blood to atone for the sins of humanity.

In Exodus 12, during the time of the Israelites' captivity in Egypt, the blood of a spotless lamb marked the doors of the faithful, protecting them from the angel of death. Similarly, the Blood of Jesus serves as our eternal

Passover lamb, shielding us from the eternal consequences of sin and offering us divine protection.

The Multifaceted Power of the Blood

The Blood of Jesus is not a mere symbol; it is a living, dynamic force with multifaceted power. Let us explore the various aspects of its divine protection:

1. Redemption and Forgiveness: When we plead the blood, we acknowledge the forgiveness of our sins through Christ's sacrifice. It cleanses us from all unrighteousness and assures us of our standing as children of God.

2. Covenant and Covering: The blood establishes a covenant between God and His people. It marks us as His own, and as we apply it in faith, it acts as a spiritual shield, covering us from harm.

3. Defeating the Accuser: Satan, the accuser of the brethren, is silenced when we plead the blood. It serves as evidence of our justification, rendering his accusations powerless.

4. Healing and Restoration: The healing power of the blood is not limited to physical ailments but extends to emotional and spiritual wounds. As we apply it, we can experience inner healing and restoration.

5. Protection from Evil Forces: Pleading the blood creates a spiritual barrier that evil forces cannot penetrate. It is our defense against spiritual attacks and demonic oppression.

The Act of Pleading the Blood

Pleading the blood is not a mere ritual; it is a declaration of faith and a powerful spiritual weapon. Here's how to effectively apply it in your life:

1. Covering Your Loved Ones: As a midnight warrior, take time to plead the blood over your family, friends, and loved ones. Declare their protection and salvation in Jesus' name.

2. Spiritual Warfare: When engaged in spiritual warfare, envision the blood of Jesus as a forcefield around you. Declare that no weapon formed against you shall prosper.

3. Breaking Generational Curses: Plead the blood to break generational curses that may have plagued your family for generations. Declare freedom and cleansing through Christ.

4. Healing and Restoration: If you are facing physical or emotional challenges, apply the blood for healing and restoration. Believe that by His stripes, you are healed.

5. Daily Declaration: Make pleading the blood a daily practice. Cover your day, your endeavors, and your interactions with the protection of the blood of Jesus.

Walking in Faith and Authority

To truly harness the power of pleading the blood, it must be coupled with unwavering faith and authority in Christ. Understand that you are not invoking a magical incantation but relying on the finished work of the Cross. Your authority as a believer enables you to command the protection and benefits of the blood.

When you plead the blood, you are declaring your allegiance to the King of Kings and Lord of Lords. You are standing on the unshakable foundation of His sacrifice. You are claiming your inheritance as a child of God, and you are putting the enemy on notice that you are covered by the blood.

The Invincible Weapon

In the midnight hour, as you face the powers of darkness and disrupt their activities, remember that the blood of Jesus is your invincible weapon. It is a weapon that transcends time and space, reaching into the heavenly realms and confounding the forces of evil. It is a weapon that is yours to wield, a weapon of divine protection and victory.

So, midnight warrior, take up the banner of the blood. Plead it over your life, your loved ones, and your spiritual battles. Let it be the crimson shield that guards your heart and soul. In the name of Jesus, let the enemy know that you are covered by the Blood of the Lamb, and no weapon formed against you shall prosper. As you do, you will walk in the divine protection and authority that is your birthright as a child of the Most High God.

Warfare Prayer

1. In the name of Jesus, I declare the power of the Blood of Jesus over my life, covering me from head to toe.

2. By the Blood of the Lamb, I am redeemed, and my sins are forgiven. I stand justified before God.

3. I plead the Blood of Jesus over my loved ones, declaring their salvation and protection.

4. Every accusation of the enemy against me is null and void, for I am covered by the Blood.

5. I declare that the Blood of Jesus creates a spiritual barrier around me, keeping evil forces at bay.

6. In Jesus' name, I break every generational curse by the power of His Blood.

7. By His stripes, I am healed. I declare divine health and restoration over my body, mind, and soul.

8. I plead the Blood over my home, declaring it a place of peace, love, and divine presence.

9. No weapon formed against me shall prosper, for I am protected by the Blood of Jesus.

10. I take authority over every demonic attack and disruption in my life, commanding them to flee in Jesus' name.

11. I declare that the Blood of Jesus purifies and cleanses me from all unrighteousness.

12. I plead the Blood over my finances, declaring God's provision and abundance.

13. I cover my mind with the Blood of Jesus, declaring protection against negative thoughts and fears.

14. I release the power of the Blood over my dreams and visions, that they may align with God's purpose for my life.

15. In Jesus' name, I declare that the Blood shields me from accidents and harm.

16. I break every stronghold and bondage in my life by the power of the Blood.

17. I plead the Blood over my relationships, declaring unity, love, and reconciliation.

18. I command every spirit of fear and anxiety to leave in Jesus' name, for I am covered by the Blood.

19. I release the angels of God to encamp around me, guarding and protecting me day and night.

20. I declare that the Blood of Jesus is a forcefield around my home, keeping it safe from all harm.

21. By the Blood, I am more than a conqueror in every situation and circumstance.

22. I plead the Blood over my purpose and destiny, declaring divine guidance and fulfillment.

23. Every plot and scheme of the enemy against me is exposed and defeated by the Blood of Jesus.

24. I declare that I walk in divine favor and blessing because of the Blood.

25. I take authority over sickness and disease, commanding them to leave my body in Jesus' name.

26. By the Blood, I am set free from the bondage of sin and addiction.

27. I declare that I am a warrior of the midnight hour, armed with the Blood of Jesus and the authority of His name.

28. I plead the Blood over my children, declaring their safety and godly upbringing.

29. I release the power of the Blood to heal and restore every broken area of my life.

30. I command every storm in my life to be calm in Jesus' name, for the Blood speaks peace.

31. I plead the Blood over my words and actions, that they may bring glory to God.

32. In Jesus' name, I break every curse spoken against me, for the Blood nullifies their power.

33. I declare that the Blood of Jesus is my banner of victory, and I will not be defeated.

34. I release the power of the Blood to open doors of opportunity and divine connections.

35. I take authority over every hindrance and obstacle in my path, commanding them to be removed by the Blood.

36. I plead the Blood over my spiritual discernment, that I may recognize and expose the enemy's tactics.

37. By the Blood, I am an overcomer, and I triumph over every challenge that comes my way.

38. I declare that the Blood of Jesus empowers me to live a life of holiness and righteousness.

39. I cover my dreams and aspirations with the Blood, believing that God's plans for me will come to pass.

40. In Jesus' name, I seal these declarations with the Blood of the Lamb, knowing that they are established in heaven and on earth. Amen

Chapter 5

Decrees of Authority:
Taking Dominion at Midnight

In the world of spiritual warfare, the midnight hour holds a unique significance. It is the time when the realms of the natural and supernatural intersect, and a powerful opportunity for believers to exercise their authority in Christ. In this chapter, we will delve deep into the concept of decrees of authority and how they play a pivotal role in taking dominion at midnight from a Christian perspective.

The Midnight Hour: A Gateway to the Spiritual Realm

Midnight is not just a random moment on the clock; it is a divine appointment with the supernatural. Throughout the Bible, we find instances where midnight was a time of divine intervention. One of the most notable examples is found in Acts 16:25-26, where Paul and Silas, imprisoned in the darkest of dungeons, chose to worship and pray at midnight. Their prayers and praises triggered a seismic shift in the spiritual realm, shaking the foundations of the prison and setting them free. This powerful event demonstrates that the midnight hour is a strategic moment when God's power is unleashed.

Understanding Decrees of Authority

Decrees of authority are bold, declarative statements made by believers who understand their position in Christ. They are not mere wishes or pleas; they are proclamations of the will of God. When we make decrees of authority, we are aligning our words with God's Word, tapping into His promises, and exercising the authority given to us by Jesus Himself.

The Source of Authority

Before we delve deeper into the practice of making decrees of authority, it's essential to understand the source of our authority. As Christians, our authority is not self-generated; it flows from our identity in Christ. Jesus, the King of Kings and Lord of Lords, has given us the authority to act in His name. In Luke 10:19, He says, "Behold, I have given you authority to tread on serpents and scorpions, and over all the power of the enemy, and nothing shall hurt you."

Decrees of Authority and the Word of God

Decrees of authority find their foundation in the Word of God. In Psalm 103:20-21, we are reminded that angels heed the voice of God's Word. When we align our decrees with Scripture, we release the power of God's Word into the spiritual realm. For example, if you are facing fear, you can decree, "For God has not given me a spirit of fear, but of power, love, and a sound mind" (2 Timothy 1:7). This decree not only proclaims God's truth but also rebukes the spirit of fear.

Keys to Effective Decrees of Authority

1. Faith-Filled Declarations: Decrees of authority must be made in faith. Hebrews 11:6 tells us that without faith, it is impossible to please God. When we declare God's promises with unwavering faith, we activate the supernatural.

2. Alignment with God's Will: Effective decrees align with God's will. As John writes in 1 John 5:14, "And this is the confidence that we have toward him, that if we ask anything according to his will, he hears us." Seek His will through prayer and Scripture.

3. Persistence: Just as Paul and Silas continued to pray and praise at midnight, we should persist in our decrees. Jesus encouraged persistence in prayer in Luke 18:1-8, emphasizing the need to keep pressing in.

4. Unity: There is power in agreement. Matthew 18:19-20 teaches us that when two or more agree on anything in Jesus' name, it will be done. Engage in corporate decrees with fellow believers for greater impact.

Decrees for Different Battlefronts

Decrees of authority can be tailored to specific areas of spiritual warfare. Here are some examples:

1. Decrees for Personal Victory: "I decree victory over every addiction, stronghold, and bondage in the name of Jesus. I am more than a conqueror through Christ who strengthens me."

2. Decrees for Family Restoration: "I decree the salvation and reconciliation of every member of my family. As for me and my house, we will serve the Lord."

3. Decrees for Healing: "I decree divine health and healing in my body. By the stripes of Jesus, I am healed, and no sickness or disease shall prosper against me."

4. Decrees for Spiritual Awakening: "I decree a mighty outpouring of the Holy Spirit in my community. The lost will be saved, the captives set free, and revival will sweep through this land."

The Impact of Midnight Decrees

When we make decrees of authority at midnight, we are engaging in a divine partnership with God. These decrees have the power to:

- Shift spiritual atmospheres.
- Break the chains of oppression.

- Release angelic reinforcements.
- Confound the plans of the enemy.
- Establish God's kingdom on earth.

Putting It into Practice

To take dominion at midnight, set aside time each night to make decrees of authority. Find a quiet place, open your Bible, and declare God's promises. Pray with boldness, knowing that you are seated with Christ in heavenly places (Ephesians 2:6). As you make decrees, watch expectantly for the manifestation of God's power in your life and in the lives of those you are interceding for.

Decrees of authority are not empty words; they are powerful weapons in the arsenal of the midnight warrior. By understanding the source of our authority, aligning with God's Word, and practicing faith-filled declarations, we can take dominion at midnight and see the kingdom of God advance in unprecedented ways. As you continue on your midnight warfare journey, remember that you are not alone; the King of Glory is with you, and through Him, you can overcome all the powers of darkness.

Warfare Prayer

1. In the mighty name of Jesus, I declare my authority over the darkness of the midnight hour.

2. By the power of the Holy Spirit within me, I take dominion at midnight over every spiritual realm.

3. I decree that my words are filled with faith, and they release the supernatural into my life.

4. In Jesus' name, I bind and rebuke all powers of darkness that oppose God's will for my life.

5. I declare that I am a child of the Most High God, and I walk in divine authority.

6. By the authority of Christ, I break every chain of bondage in my life and in the lives of my loved ones.

7. I decree victory over every addiction, stronghold, and negative habit in my life.

8. In the name of Jesus, I command every spirit of fear to flee from my presence.

9. I declare that I am more than a conqueror through Christ who strengthens me.

10. By the stripes of Jesus, I am healed, and no sickness or disease shall prosper against me.

11. I decree divine health and vitality in my body, mind, and spirit.

12. In the authority of Jesus, I release a spirit of love, unity, and forgiveness in my family.

13. I declare the salvation and reconciliation of every member of my family.

14. As for me and my house, we will serve the Lord and walk in His ways.

15. I take authority over every financial struggle and declare abundance and prosperity in my life.

16. In the name of Jesus, I rebuke all forms of spiritual oppression and declare my freedom.

17. I release the power of the Holy Spirit to transform my thought life and renew my mind.

18. By the authority of Christ, I command every demonic influence to be silenced in my life.

19. I decree a mighty outpouring of the Holy Spirit in my community and revival in my land.

20. In Jesus' name, I release the angels of God to surround and protect me and my loved ones.

21. I take authority over every storm and declare peace in the midst of chaos.

22. By the power of God's Word, I declare that no weapon formed against me shall prosper.

23. I release supernatural wisdom, knowledge, and understanding in every area of my life.

24. I command every door of opportunity to open in God's perfect timing.

25. In the authority of Jesus, I break generational curses and declare blessings over my lineage.

26. I decree that my prayers are powerful and effective, and they bring about change in the spiritual realm.

27. By the blood of Jesus, I am covered and protected from all harm.

28. I declare that I am a warrior of light, dispelling darkness wherever I go.

29. In Jesus' name, I bind the spirits of doubt and unbelief and release unwavering faith.

30. I take authority over every assignment of the enemy and cancel their plans.

31. By the authority of Christ, I speak life and blessing over my relationships.

32. I release a spirit of unity and love in my church and among fellow believers.

33. In the name of Jesus, I break every stronghold of addiction and declare freedom.

34. I decree that my words bring encouragement and healing to those around me.

35. By the power of the Holy Spirit, I am bold and fearless in my faith.

36. I take authority over every hindrance to my spiritual growth and declare growth and maturity.

37. In Jesus' name, I release divine favor and open doors of opportunity in my career.

38. I declare that I am a vessel of God's love and a beacon of His light in the world.

39. By the authority of Christ, I bind the spirit of complacency and stir up passion for God's kingdom.

40. I take dominion at midnight and declare that the kingdom of God is advancing in my life and in the lives of those I pray for.

Chapter 6

The Midnight Watch:
Vigilance in Spiritual Warfare

In the quiet of the night, when the world is cloaked in darkness, the midnight hour beckons warriors of the faith to rise. It is a time when the physical and spiritual realms converge, and the battle between light and darkness intensifies. In this chapter, we delve deep into the concept of the midnight watch, exploring its significance, strategies, and the profound impact it can have on your spiritual warfare journey.

The Mystery of Midnight

Midnight holds a unique place in the realm of spirituality. In the Bible, midnight often marks pivotal moments of divine intervention. It was at midnight that Paul and Silas prayed and sang hymns in the depths of a prison cell, resulting in a miraculous earthquake and their liberation (Acts 16:25-26). Similarly, the Passover, a central event in the Old Testament, began at midnight when the angel of death passed over the homes marked with the blood of the lamb.

Midnight represents the darkest point in the natural world, but it is also the hour when God's light shines brightest. It is a time of transition, a bridge between one day and the next, symbolizing the breaking of old cycles and the birth of new beginnings. As midnight warriors, we tap into this spiritual significance, positioning ourselves for divine encounters and breakthroughs.

The Vigilant Warrior

To fully embrace the midnight watch, one must adopt the mindset of a vigilant warrior. Vigilance is the unwavering focus on detecting and responding to potential threats. In the spiritual realm, this means being acutely aware of the enemy's schemes and staying alert to discern God's guidance.

1. Spiritual Discernment: Vigilance begins with discernment. As a midnight warrior, you must cultivate a deep sensitivity to the Holy Spirit's leading. Discernment enables you to distinguish between the voice of God and the whispers of the adversary. It empowers you to recognize spiritual atmospheres and discern the presence of angelic or demonic forces.

2. Watchful Prayer: Prayer is the heartbeat of spiritual warfare, and in the midnight watch, it becomes a powerful weapon. The watchful warrior engages in fervent, targeted prayer. This is not a time for casual or routine prayers but a passionate pursuit of God's presence and purpose. Praying at midnight allows you to align with the supernatural rhythms of heaven, where breakthroughs and revelations abound.

3. Strategic Positioning: Just as a soldier strategically positions themselves on the battlefield, the midnight warrior strategically positions themselves in the spiritual realm. Your posture matters. Find a quiet place where you can pray, worship, and declare God's promises. Create an atmosphere conducive to encounters with the Divine.

The Weapons of the Midnight Watch

In the midnight watch, your spiritual arsenal is filled with potent weapons:

1. The Word of God: The Bible is your sword, and in the midnight hour, it becomes a blazing beacon of truth. Declare Scriptures that pertain to your situation. Speak them boldly, for the Word of God is living and active (Hebrews 4:12).

2. Praise and Worship: Music is a powerful medium for spiritual warfare. Engage in worship that exalts God and invites His presence. Your praises are like arrows that pierce the darkness.

3. Intercession: Stand in the gap for others. Intercede for your family, community, and nation. The midnight hour is a time when the cries of the righteous can shift the course of history.

4. Decrees and Declarations: Prophetic decrees release God's purposes into the earth. As a midnight warrior, boldly declare God's promises over your life and circumstances. Your words have the power to shape reality.

Navigating the Midnight Watch

Navigating the midnight watch requires discipline and commitment. Here are some practical tips:

1. Establish a Routine: Consistency is key. Set aside specific nights for your midnight watch. This routine helps you build spiritual momentum over time.

2. Fasting: Consider incorporating fasting into your midnight watch. Fasting sharpens your spiritual senses and intensifies your focus on prayer.

3. Community: Don't journey alone. Seek out fellow midnight warriors who can join you in prayer and worship. Corporate prayer amplifies your impact.

4. Journaling: Keep a journal to record your encounters and insights during the midnight watch. This creates a record of God's faithfulness and allows you to track your spiritual growth.

Rise, O Midnight Warrior

The midnight watch is not for the faint of heart. It requires dedication, fervency, and unwavering faith. But in the stillness of the night, as you watch and pray, you become a beacon of light in a world shrouded in darkness. You align with the divine purposes of God and unleash His power into the earth.

So, rise, O midnight warrior, for the battle is fierce, but the victory is assured. Embrace the mystery of midnight, walk in vigilant faith, and watch as the powers of darkness crumble in the presence of the Almighty. Your journey as a midnight warrior has just begun, and the world will never be the same.

Warfare Prayer

1. By the authority of Jesus Christ, I declare that the midnight hour is a sacred time for divine encounters and breakthroughs.

2. In Jesus' name, I declare that I am a vigilant warrior, discerning and resisting every scheme of the enemy.

3. I decree that my spiritual eyes are opened to perceive the hidden realms of the supernatural, and I walk in discernment and wisdom.

4. By the blood of Jesus, I break every chain of darkness that seeks to bind me or hinder my prayers.

5. I declare that I am a watchful warrior, standing guard over my family and loved ones in prayer.

6. In the name of Jesus, I release the power of God's Word as a two-edged sword to cut through every spiritual opposition.

7. I decree that my prayers at midnight create divine earthquakes in the spiritual realm, shaking the foundations of the enemy's strongholds.

8. By the authority of Jesus' name, I take dominion over every demonic force that opposes God's will in my life.

9. I declare that I am an overcomer, and no weapon formed against me shall prosper.

10. In Jesus' name, I bind and cast out every spirit of fear, doubt, and confusion from my mind.

11. I decree that I am filled with the Holy Spirit's power and boldness to confront the powers of darkness.

12. By the blood of Jesus, I plead divine protection over my home, covering it with the shield of faith.

13. I declare that my praises rise as a sweet aroma before God's throne, ushering in His presence.

14. In the name of Jesus, I rebuke every hindering spirit and declare an open heaven over my life.

15. I decree that I walk in the supernatural, performing signs and wonders in the name of Jesus.

16. By the authority of Christ, I break the yoke of every generational curse in my bloodline.

17. I declare that I am a night watchman, interceding for the needs of others and releasing God's blessings.

18. In Jesus' name, I release ministering angels to go forth and execute God's assignments on my behalf.

19. I decree that every stronghold in my life is demolished, and I am free in Christ.

20. By the blood of the Lamb, I plead for the salvation of souls in my family and community.

21. I declare that my dreams and visions are filled with divine revelation and insight.

22. In the name of Jesus, I bind and rebuke every spirit of deception that seeks to confuse my path.

23. I decree that I am a vessel of honor, set apart for God's glory and purposes.

24. By the authority of Christ, I release the fire of the Holy Spirit to consume all impurities within me.

25. I declare that I am fearless, and no intimidation from the enemy can deter my mission.

26. In Jesus' name, I speak healing and restoration into every area of my life and body.

27. I decree that I walk in victory, for greater is He who is in me than he who is in the world.

28. By the blood of Jesus, I plead divine favor and open doors for God's kingdom advancement.

29. I declare that I am a history-maker, influencing the course of events through my prayers.

30. In the name of Jesus, I rebuke every storm of life, and I command peace and calm.

31. I decree that I am anointed for the midnight hour, and my prayers are effective and powerful.

32. By the authority of Christ, I declare that my family is a stronghold of faith and love.

33. I declare that my worship and adoration of God release His glory and presence into my life.

34. In Jesus' name, I rebuke every attack on my identity and declare my true worth in Christ.

35. I decree that I am a vessel of honor, carrying the light of Christ into every dark corner.

36. By the blood of Jesus, I plead for the restoration of prodigals and the lost.

37. I declare that I am a voice in the wilderness, preparing the way for the Lord's return.

38. In the name of Jesus, I release divine creativity and innovation into my endeavors.

39. I decree that I am a history-maker, leaving a legacy of faith and courage.

40. By the authority of Christ, I seal these declarations, knowing that God's purposes will be fulfilled in my life and in the midnight watch. Amen.

Chapter 7

Breaking Chains and Shackles:
Freedom Declarations

In the dimly lit hours of the midnight watch, a profound spiritual battle unfolds. It is a battle for freedom—a battle to break the chains and shackles that bind our lives, our minds, and our souls. This chapter delves deeply into the transformative power of Freedom Declarations, exploring the profound impact they can have on our lives from a Christian perspective. Prepare to journey into the heart of spiritual warfare and discover how you can unleash the might of your faith to shatter the bonds that have held you captive.

The Nature of Chains and Shackles

Before we dive into the heart of Freedom Declarations, it is essential to understand the nature of the chains and shackles we face in our lives. These bonds are not merely physical; they are often spiritual and emotional, ensnaring us in a web of despair, fear, and hopelessness. They manifest as addictions, destructive habits, and toxic thought patterns, keeping us from living the abundant life that Christ promised.

Chains and shackles can take various forms, such as:

1. Addictions: Whether it's substance abuse, gambling, or any other compulsive behavior, addictions grip us tightly, making us feel powerless.

2. Emotional Bondage: Unresolved trauma, bitterness, and unforgiveness can chain us to our past, preventing us from moving forward in freedom.

3. Demonic Oppression: Spiritual forces of darkness can exert control over our lives, causing spiritual bondage that keeps us from experiencing God's fullness.

4. Fear and Anxiety: Anxiety can be a paralyzing shackle, keeping us from pursuing God's plans and purpose for our lives.

The Power of Declarations

Freedom Declarations are more than just words; they are weapons of spiritual warfare. When you declare your freedom in the name of Jesus, you are aligning your words with the authority of Christ Himself. This is a practice deeply rooted in Christian faith, and it is a direct response to the teachings of the Bible.

"So if the Son sets you free, you will be free indeed." (John 8:36)

"I can do all things through Him who strengthens me." (Philippians 4:13)

"For God gave us a spirit not of fear but of power and love and self-control." (2 Timothy 1:7)

These verses emphasize the power and authority that believers possess through their faith in Christ. Freedom Declarations serve as a tangible expression of that faith. When spoken with conviction and belief, they can break the chains and shackles that have held you captive for far too long.

Crafting Your Freedom Declarations

Freedom Declarations should be personal and specific. They are not generic affirmations but rather laser-focused declarations of your intent to break free from a particular area of bondage. Here's a step-by-step guide on how to craft your Freedom Declarations:

1. Identify the Bondage: Start by pinpointing the specific chains and shackles that have been limiting your life. Is it an addiction, fear, or emotional trauma? Be honest with yourself.

2. Consult Scripture: Search the Bible for verses that address your particular area of bondage. Find promises and declarations of freedom that resonate with you.

3. Personalize Your Declaration: Craft a declaration that is personal to you. For example, if you're battling addiction, your declaration might be, "In the name of Jesus, I declare my freedom from the bondage of [specific

addiction]. I am no longer a slave to this, for whom the Son sets free is free indeed."

4. Speak with Conviction: When you declare your freedom, do it with unwavering faith and conviction. Speak as if you believe it with all your heart, for faith is the key that unlocks the power of these declarations.

Breaking the Chains in Practice

Now that you have your Freedom Declaration, it's time to put it into action. Here's a practical guide on how to use your declaration to break the chains:

1. Set Aside Time: Find a quiet and undisturbed place where you can engage in prayer and declaration. Midnight is often seen as a powerful time for spiritual warfare, but you can do this at any time that suits you.

2. Begin in Worship: Start by worshiping God and acknowledging His sovereignty. This sets the spiritual atmosphere for your declaration.

3. Declare Your Freedom: Speak your Freedom Declaration aloud, multiple times if necessary. Let the power of your words resonate in the spiritual realm.

4. Invoke the Name of Jesus: Throughout your declaration, invoke the name of Jesus. It is through His name that chains are shattered.

5. Believe and Receive: As you declare your freedom, believe that it is done. Receive your freedom by faith. Thank God for His deliverance.

The Battle Continues

It's important to understand that breaking chains and shackles is often not a one-time event. Spiritual warfare can be an ongoing battle. There may be times when you need to reaffirm your Freedom Declaration and stand strong in your faith. The enemy may attempt to re-ensnare you, but remember that you have the authority and power to resist.

In the darkest moments of your midnight battle, remember this: Freedom Declarations are not just words; they are conduits of God's divine power. They are the keys that unlock the prison doors of bondage, and they are your declaration of independence from the powers of darkness.

As you continue your journey into spiritual warfare, know that you are not alone. The midnight warriors, united in prayer and faith, are a formidable force against the powers of darkness. In the chapters ahead, we will delve deeper into specific areas of bondage and provide you with more Freedom Declarations tailored to your needs. But for now, declare your freedom with boldness and conviction, for the chains are already breaking, and the shackles are falling away.

Warfare Prayer

1. In the mighty name of Jesus, I declare that every chain of addiction in my life is shattered, and I am free indeed!

2. Lord Jesus, I declare my freedom from fear and anxiety. Your perfect love casts out all fear.

3. By the authority of Christ, I break the shackles of past trauma and declare my healing and restoration.

4. In Jesus' name, I declare my release from every demonic oppression that has hindered my life.

5. I take authority in the name of Jesus over every generational curse, and I declare my family's freedom.

6. Lord, I declare that my mind is renewed by your Word, and I am free from negative thought patterns.

7. By the power of the Holy Spirit, I break the chains of bitterness and unforgiveness in my heart.

8. In Jesus' name, I declare that I am no longer a slave to sin but a servant of righteousness.

Chapter 8

The Power of Fasting:
Strengthening Your Spiritual Arsenal

In the realm of spiritual warfare, fasting is a formidable weapon that can strengthen your spiritual arsenal like no other. It is a practice deeply rooted in Christian tradition, with its roots tracing back to the Bible itself. Fasting is not merely a physical discipline; it is a spiritual exercise that can unlock incredible spiritual power, enhance your discernment, and bring about transformation in your life. In this chapter, we will delve into the profound significance of fasting, its various forms, and how it can empower you to become a midnight warrior of exceptional strength and clarity.

The Ancient Art of Fasting

Fasting is not a trendy diet or a passing health fad; it is a sacred act of self-denial and devotion. Its roots in Christianity can be found in the Old Testament, where it was practiced by prophets, leaders, and devoted followers of God. Moses, Elijah, Daniel, and Esther are just a few of the biblical figures who engaged in fasting during times of great need and spiritual warfare.

Fasting involves abstaining from food, and sometimes even water, for a set period. While it may seem extreme, it serves a profound purpose – to shift your focus from the physical to the spiritual, to humble oneself before God, and to seek His guidance, deliverance, and intervention in times of crisis.

Types of Fasting

1. Normal Fast: This is the complete abstention from food for a specific period while still consuming water. It is a common form of fasting.

2. Absolute Fast: This is the most intense form of fasting, involving abstaining from both food and water. It's rarely practiced and should be approached with caution due to its extreme nature.

3. Partial Fast: In this form, individuals limit their diet by excluding certain foods or meals while maintaining some level of sustenance. An example is the Daniel Fast, which omits meat, sweets, and other specific foods.

4. Intermittent Fast: This fasting method alternates between periods of eating and fasting. While it's often used for physical health benefits, it can also be adapted for spiritual purposes.

Fasting in Spiritual Warfare

1. Heightened Spiritual Sensitivity:

Fasting helps to sharpen your spiritual senses. When your physical appetites are subdued, your spiritual senses become more acute. This heightened sensitivity enables you to discern the spiritual realm more clearly and perceive the schemes of the enemy.

2. Breaking Strongholds:

Fasting is a powerful tool for breaking strongholds and chains that may have bound you for years. It is a declaration of your dependence on God and a renunciation of the enemy's hold on your life. As you fast and pray, these strongholds begin to crumble.

3. Spiritual Clarity:

The fog of confusion and doubt often obscures our understanding of God's will. Fasting brings clarity. It aligns your heart with God's purposes, enabling you to hear His voice and receive guidance with unprecedented clarity.

4. Intimacy with God:

Fasting is a profound act of worship and intimacy with God. It is a time to draw near to Him, to seek His face, and to deepen your relationship. As you deny yourself physically, you become more open to His presence and His revelation.

5. Empowering Your Prayers:

When combined with prayer, fasting supercharges your prayers. Your petitions become fervent and effective. You are no longer praying from a place of weakness but from a position of strength and authority.

Practical Tips for Fasting

1. Start Small: If you're new to fasting, begin with a short fast, perhaps skipping one meal. Gradually increase the duration as you become more comfortable with the practice.

2. Set Clear Goals: Determine the purpose of your fast. Are you seeking guidance, deliverance, or breakthrough? Having a clear goal will give your fast direction and focus.

3. Spiritual Preparation: Before and during your fast, engage in fervent prayer, Bible study, and worship. Use this time to draw closer to God.

4. Breaking the Fast: When ending a fast, do so gradually and with care. Start with easily digestible foods and gradually reintroduce your regular diet.

Real-Life Testimonies

To illustrate the transformative power of fasting, here are a few real-life testimonies of individuals who have experienced remarkable breakthroughs through fasting:

Testimony 1: Mary's Deliverance

Mary was battling with addiction for years. She turned to fasting and prayer, seeking deliverance from this stronghold. Through a 21-day fast, she not only overcame her addiction but also found renewed strength and purpose in her life.

Testimony 2: John's Clarity

John was facing a major life decision and was uncertain about the right path. He embarked on a three-day fast to seek God's guidance. During this time, he received a clear vision of his calling and stepped into a new season of purpose and fulfillment.

Testimony 3: Sarah's Healing

Sarah had been struggling with a chronic illness. Frustrated by the lack of medical solutions, she embarked on a 40-day fast, believing in God's healing power. Miraculously, her health improved, and she experienced complete healing.

Fasting is not a magic formula, but it is a powerful spiritual discipline that can revolutionize your spiritual warfare efforts. As you commit to fasting, you position yourself as a midnight warrior of extraordinary strength and clarity. It is a journey of self-denial, spiritual intimacy, and empowerment that will equip you to confront the powers of darkness with unwavering faith and authority. In the darkest hours of the night, your fast becomes a beacon of light and a declaration of victory.

Warfare Prayer

1. In the name of Jesus, I declare that as I fast, my spiritual sensitivity is heightened, and I discern the enemy's schemes with clarity.

2. By the authority of Jesus Christ, I break every stronghold and chain that has bound me, and I walk in freedom through fasting.

3. Heavenly Father, I declare that fasting brings spiritual clarity, and I align my heart with your will to hear your voice clearly.

4. In the name of Jesus, I declare that my fasting is an act of worship and intimacy with God, drawing me nearer to His presence.

5. By the authority of Jesus' name, I declare that my prayers during fasting are fervent and effective, bringing forth supernatural breakthroughs.

6. Lord, I declare that I start small in fasting, and by your grace, I will increase my fasting duration over time.

7. In the name of Jesus, I declare that I will stay hydrated during my fasts to maintain physical and spiritual strength.

8. Heavenly Father, I set clear goals for my fasting, seeking your guidance, deliverance, and breakthroughs in specific areas of my life.

9. By the authority of Jesus Christ, I declare that I am spiritually prepared through prayer, Bible study, and worship before and during my fasts.

10. In the name of Jesus, I declare that when I break my fast, it is done gradually and with care, following wise dietary practices.

11. Lord, I thank you for the transformative power of fasting in my life and declare that I will experience breakthroughs in every area of my journey.

12. By the authority of Jesus' name, I declare that every addiction and stronghold in my life is broken through fasting and the power of the Holy Spirit.

13. Heavenly Father, I declare that as I fast, I receive divine guidance and clarity for every decision and crossroads in my life.

14. In the name of Jesus, I declare that my health is restored and renewed through fasting, and I walk in divine healing and wholeness.

15. By the authority of Jesus Christ, I declare that my fast is a spiritual weapon that disarms the enemy and brings forth victory in every battle.

16. Lord, I declare that as I fast, my hunger for you and your Word deepens, and I hunger and thirst for righteousness.

17. In the name of Jesus, I declare that I am a midnight warrior of extraordinary strength and authority through fasting and prayer.

18. By the authority of Jesus' name, I declare that the darkness flees before the light of my fast, and I walk in victory over the powers of darkness.

19. Heavenly Father, I declare that I am a vessel of your glory, and my fasts release your glory and power into every situation.

20. In the name of Jesus, I declare that I am a warrior of faith, and my fasting builds unshakable faith in the promises of God.

21. By the authority of Jesus Christ, I declare that I am clothed in the full armor of God, and my fasting fortifies my spiritual defenses.

22. Lord, I declare that fasting makes me an instrument of righteousness and holiness, and I am set apart for Your divine purposes.

23. In the name of Jesus, I declare that I am a watchman on the wall, and my fasts release divine protection over my life and loved ones.

24. By the authority of Jesus' name, I declare that my fasts break generational curses, and I walk in generational blessings and favor.

25. Heavenly Father, I declare that I am a carrier of revival, and my fasts ignite revival fires in my community and nation.

26. In the name of Jesus, I declare that I am a vessel of reconciliation, and my fasts bring healing and unity to broken relationships.

27. By the authority of Jesus Christ, I declare that my fasts release supernatural provision and abundance in every area of my life.

28. Lord, I declare that I am an overcomer, and my fasts empower me to overcome every trial and tribulation.

29. In the name of Jesus, I declare that I am a light in the darkness, and my fasts shine brightly, dispelling the works of darkness.

30. By the authority of Jesus' name, I declare that my fasts bring restoration and redemption to areas of my life that have been broken and lost.

31. Heavenly Father, I declare that I am a vessel of compassion, and my fasts lead me to serve and love others selflessly.

32. In the name of Jesus, I declare that my fasts release divine wisdom and discernment, enabling me to make wise and godly decisions.

33. By the authority of Jesus Christ, I declare that my fasts break down the walls of division and hatred, and I walk in love and unity with others.

34. Lord, I declare that my fasts release miracles and signs that testify to your greatness and power.

35. In the name of Jesus, I declare that my fasts bring forth supernatural favor and open doors that no man can shut.

36. By the authority of Jesus' name, I declare that I am an ambassador of the Kingdom of God, and my fasts advance His Kingdom on earth.

37. Heavenly Father, I declare that I am an intercessor, and my fasts carry the burdens of others before your throne of grace.

38. In the name of Jesus, I declare that my fasts release divine restoration and reconciliation in broken families.

39. By the authority of Jesus Christ, I declare that my fasts dismantle the strongholds of addiction and bring deliverance to the captives.

40. Lord, I declare that my fasts are a testimony of your faithfulness, and I will continue to fast and pray, knowing that you are with me,

strengthening my spiritual arsenal, and leading me to victory in every battle. Amen.

Chapter 9

Divine Firestorms:
Praying with Holy Boldness

In the realm of spiritual warfare, there exists a divine weapon that few warriors dare to wield: the firestorm of holy boldness. As midnight warriors, our prayers are not mere requests whispered timidly into the night; they are declarations of spiritual authority, thundering proclamations that shake the very foundations of the heavenly and earthly realms. In this chapter, we will delve deep into the concept of divine firestorms and how to pray with holy boldness, igniting a spiritual revolution that disrupts the activities of darkness.

The Nature of Holy Boldness

Before we can grasp the power of holy boldness, we must understand its nature. Holy boldness is not arrogance or pride but an unwavering confidence in the promises and authority bestowed upon us by our heavenly Father. It is rooted in a profound understanding of our identity as children of God and co-heirs with Christ. In Ephesians 3:12, we are reminded, "In him and through faith in him, we may approach God with freedom and confidence." This freedom and confidence are the essence of holy boldness.

The Source of Holy Boldness

To pray with holy boldness, we must draw from the divine source of boldness: the Holy Spirit. Acts 4:31 recounts the disciples' experience: "After they prayed, the place where they were meeting was shaken. And they were all filled with the Holy Spirit and spoke the word of God boldly." When we allow the Holy Spirit to fill us, we are infused with the boldness to speak and pray with authority.

Praying with Holy Boldness

1. Identity Affirmation: Holy boldness begins with knowing who you are in Christ. Before entering into prayer, affirm your identity as a child of God, clothed in the righteousness of Christ. Declare your position as an heir to the promises of God.

2. Scriptural Foundation: Ground your prayers in the Word of God. Identify promises, declarations, and principles in Scripture that pertain to your situation. When you pray in alignment with God's Word, your boldness is anchored in truth.

3. Renounce Fear: Boldness and fear cannot coexist. As you enter into prayer, renounce all fear, doubt, and unbelief. Speak against any spirit of timidity and declare your trust in God's faithfulness.

4. Prophetic Declarations: Release prophetic declarations over your situation. Proclaim God's will with unwavering certainty. Declare victory, healing, deliverance, and restoration as if they were already manifested in the natural realm.

5. Spiritual Warfare: Engage in spiritual warfare with holy aggression. Command the powers of darkness to flee, break their strongholds, and disrupt their activities. Your words are like spiritual fire, consuming the enemy's plans.

6. Passionate Worship: Combine your prayers with passionate worship. As you worship in spirit and truth, the atmosphere becomes charged with the presence of God, intensifying the impact of your bold prayers.

7. Persistent Intercession: Holy boldness is not a one-time event but a lifestyle of persistent intercession. Maintain your boldness even in the face of apparent setbacks. Your unwavering faith will lead to breakthroughs.

Case Studies of Holy Boldness

Let's explore a few inspiring case studies of individuals who exemplified holy boldness in their prayers:

- Daniel in the Lion's Den: Daniel's unwavering trust in God led him to pray boldly despite the threat of lions. His faith disrupted the plans of his adversaries and resulted in a miraculous deliverance (Daniel 6:16-23).

- Elijah on Mount Carmel: Elijah's bold challenge to the prophets of Baal on Mount Carmel showcased the power of praying with holy boldness. Fire fell from heaven, affirming the supremacy of the one true God (1 Kings 18:16-40).

- The Early Church: Acts 4:29-31 records the prayers of the early church for boldness. As a result, they were filled with the Holy Spirit, and their bold witness for Christ turned the world upside down.

The Impact of Holy Boldness

Praying with holy boldness has a profound impact on the spiritual realm. It disrupts the activities of darkness, shatters strongholds, and releases the miraculous. When we pray with holy boldness, we become conduits of God's power, ushering in His kingdom on earth as it is in heaven.

In the midnight hour, when the powers of darkness are most active, the midnight warrior rises with holy boldness. They stand firm in their identity, rooted in the Word, empowered by the Spirit, and unyielding in their faith. Through divine firestorms of prayer, they declare the victory of the cross, and darkness trembles in their presence. As you embark on this journey of praying with holy boldness, remember the words of Hebrews 4:16: "Let us then approach God's throne of grace with confidence so that we may receive mercy and find grace to help us in our time of need."

Approach with confidence, for you are a Midnight Warrior—an agent of divine transformation in the midnight hour.

Warfare Prayer

1. By the authority of Jesus Christ, I declare that I am a Midnight Warrior, clothed in holy boldness to disrupt the activities of darkness.

2. In Jesus' name, I boldly declare my identity as a child of God, a co-heir with Christ, and a vessel of His power.

3. I renounce all fear, doubt, and timidity. I am filled with divine confidence to approach the throne of grace with holy boldness.

4. By the Word of God, I declare that I am more than a conqueror through Christ who strengthens me (Romans 8:37).

5. I release the fire of the Holy Spirit within me to ignite a divine firestorm in my prayers.

6. In the name of Jesus, I command every power of darkness opposing my life to scatter and be rendered powerless.

7. I proclaim victory over every spiritual battle, knowing that greater is He who is in me than he who is in the world (1 John 4:4).

8. I declare that my prayers are aligned with God's Word, and His promises are manifesting in my life.

9. I boldly decree that no weapon formed against me shall prosper, for my righteousness is from the Lord (Isaiah 54:17).

10. In Jesus' name, I rebuke sickness, infirmity, and disease. By His stripes, I am healed (Isaiah 53:5).

11. I command the restoration of what the enemy has stolen from me, sevenfold, according to God's promise (Proverbs 6:31).

12. I declare that my family is covered by the blood of Jesus, and no harm shall come near us (Psalm 91:7).

13. I release the fire of revival over my community and nation. Let hearts turn to God in repentance and faith.

14. By the authority in Jesus' name, I break every generational curse and declare freedom and blessing over my bloodline.

15. I declare that every obstacle in my path is removed, and every mountain is leveled in Jesus' name (Mark 11:23).

16. I command doors of opportunity to open for me, for God has set before me an open door that no one can shut (Revelation 3:8).

17. I declare that my prayers are like arrows of fire, piercing the darkness and bringing transformation.

18. In the name of Jesus, I bind the spirit of fear and release a spirit of power, love, and sound mind (2 Timothy 1:7).

19. I decree that the plans of the enemy are exposed and thwarted by the light of God's truth.

20. I release divine favor and blessings over my workplace, knowing that I am a light in the darkness.

21. I declare that I walk in divine wisdom and understanding, making the most of every opportunity (Ephesians 5:15-16).

22. In Jesus' name, I command peace to reign in my heart, my home, and my relationships.

23. I release the fire of revival over the church, that it may be a beacon of hope and transformation in the world.

24. I declare that I am an overcomer by the blood of the Lamb and the word of my testimony (Revelation 12:11).

25. I rebuke spiritual apathy and complacency, and I embrace a fervent spirit of prayer.

26. I declare that my prayers shift the atmosphere, releasing healing, deliverance, and breakthroughs.

27. In the name of Jesus, I release supernatural dreams and visions that align with God's purpose for my life.

28. I declare that I am a vessel of God's love, bringing reconciliation and unity wherever I go.

29. I bind the works of the enemy in my family and release God's divine order and harmony.

30. I declare that the angels of God encamp around me and my loved ones, protecting us from all harm (Psalm 34:7).

31. By the authority of Jesus' name, I release the fire of revival over my city, that it may be transformed by the love of Christ.

32. I decree that I am an instrument of peace, bringing reconciliation and healing to broken relationships.

33. I bind the spirit of division and release a spirit of unity and understanding in my church.

34. In Jesus' name, I declare that my prayers release divine solutions to complex problems.

35. I release the fire of God's presence in my worship, knowing that where the Spirit of the Lord is, there is freedom (2 Corinthians 3:17).

36. I declare that my prayers are unstoppable, for nothing is impossible with God (Luke 1:37).

37. By the authority of Jesus' name, I release divine provision and abundance over my life and ministry.

38. I command the gates of heaven to open, pouring out blessings that I cannot contain (Malachi 3:10).

39. I declare that I am a vessel of honor, sanctified and prepared for every good work (2 Timothy 2:21).

40. In Jesus' name, I seal these declarations with the blood of the Lamb, knowing that they are established in the heavenly realms. Amen and amen!

Chapter 10

Confronting Principalities:
A Midnight Battle Plan

In the realm of spiritual warfare, midnight is the sacred hour when the veil between the physical and the spiritual world is at its thinnest. It is a time when the forces of darkness are most active, but it is also a time when the midnight warriors, armed with the power of the Holy Spirit, can confront and conquer the principalities and powers that seek to oppose them. In this chapter, we will delve deep into the intricacies of confronting principalities, offering you a comprehensive midnight battle plan to face these formidable spiritual entities.

Understanding Principalities

Before we embark on our battle plan, it's crucial to understand what principalities are. In Christian theology, principalities are high-ranking demonic beings that hold authority over regions, nations, and even specific aspects of human life. These malevolent beings operate in the spiritual realm, exerting influence over governments, institutions, and individuals. They are often hidden, working in the shadows to promote darkness and hinder the advancement of God's kingdom.

The Midnight Hour: Why It Matters

The midnight hour is symbolic in spiritual warfare for several reasons. First, it aligns with the idea that darkness flees from the light. As the world sleeps, the midnight warriors rise to confront the spiritual darkness that seeks to envelope humanity. Second, midnight is a time of stillness and quiet, making it ideal for deep, focused prayer and spiritual warfare. Finally, it mirrors the concept of spiritual awakening—a call to arise from spiritual slumber and engage in the battle for souls.

Preparing for Midnight Warfare

To confront principalities effectively, you must be spiritually prepared and equipped. Here are some essential steps to consider:

1. Purification: Begin with personal purification. Confess your sins and repent of any unrighteousness in your life. Cleansing yourself spiritually is essential to ensure that your prayers are not hindered.

2. Armor Up: Put on the full armor of God (Ephesians 6:10-18). Each piece of the armor is critical for protection and offense in spiritual warfare.

3. Fasting: Consider fasting to sharpen your spiritual senses and draw closer to God. Fasting can break strongholds and prepare your heart for battle.

4. Gather Intelligence: Seek guidance from the Holy Spirit about the specific principality you are confronting. Understanding its nature and tactics will help you formulate a targeted battle plan.

Engaging in Midnight Warfare

Now, let's delve into the practical steps of confronting principalities during the midnight hour:

Step 1: Enter into Worship

Begin your midnight battle with worship. Praise and worship invite the presence of God and prepare your heart for spiritual warfare. Sing songs of victory and declare the greatness of our God.

Step 2: Praying in the Spirit

Praying in tongues, also known as praying in the Spirit, is a powerful tool in spiritual warfare. It bypasses our limited understanding and allows the Holy Spirit to intercede through us, especially when we don't know how to pray as we should (Romans 8:26-27).

Step 3: Binding and Loosing

Use the authority given to you by Christ (Matthew 16:19) to bind the principalities that oppose God's purposes and to loose the blessings and purposes of God upon the earth. Declare, "I bind every principality hindering God's will in this region, and I loose the power of God's kingdom."

Step 4: Prophetic Declarations

Speak prophetic declarations into the spiritual realm. Declare the victory of Christ over the principalities and proclaim God's sovereignty. Speak life, light, and truth into the darkness.

Step 5: Spiritual Mapping

Utilize spiritual mapping to identify specific areas or strongholds where the principality's influence is most prominent. Pray strategically for these areas, asking God to break the strongholds and release His kingdom.

Step 6: Persistent Prayer

Midnight warfare is not a one-time event but a sustained effort. Continue to pray consistently, knowing that spiritual battles may require persistence. Persevere until you see breakthrough.

Step 7: Unity in Prayer

Whenever possible, engage in corporate prayer. The power of unified prayer is immense, and it can shake the foundations of the enemy's strongholds.

Step 8: Watch and Listen

During midnight warfare, be watchful and discerning. The Holy Spirit may reveal insights, visions, or dreams that provide guidance for your battle.

Step 9: Celebrate Victory

After your midnight warfare, take time to celebrate and thank God for the victory. Recognize that you have engaged in a battle that has eternal significance.

Confronting principalities during the midnight hour is a powerful and bold endeavor. With a comprehensive battle plan that includes worship, prayer, binding and loosing, prophetic declarations, and spiritual mapping, you can effectively engage in spiritual warfare. Remember that your authority comes from Christ, and through Him, you have the power to overcome even the mightiest of principalities. Stay vigilant, stay fervent, and may the light of Christ dispel the darkness in the midnight hour.

Warfare Prayer

1. In the mighty name of Jesus, I declare that I am a Midnight Warrior, chosen and equipped for spiritual battle.

2. By the authority vested in me through Christ, I bind every principality that opposes God's will in my life, my region, and the world.

3. I loose the power of God's kingdom to reign and rule over every realm and territory under the influence of principalities.

4. I declare that the darkness is dispelled, and the light of Christ shines brightly in every area of spiritual conflict.

5. In the name of Jesus, I worship and praise the Lord, for He is the King of Kings and the Lord of Lords.

6. I pray in the Spirit, allowing the Holy Spirit to intercede through me, revealing the hidden strategies of the enemy.

7. I decree that every demonic assignment and plot orchestrated by principalities is null and void in Jesus' name.

8. By the blood of Jesus, I break every chain and stronghold established by principalities in my life and community.

9. I release the fire of the Holy Spirit to consume every principality's influence and plans in Jesus' name.

10. I prophesy victory and divine breakthrough in every area where principalities have held sway.

11. I declare that the power and authority of Christ far surpass any principality's dominion, and I stand firm in that truth.

12. In the name of Jesus, I bind the spirit of fear, doubt, and confusion that principalities may attempt to release.

13. I loose the spirit of wisdom, discernment, and revelation to guide me in confronting principalities effectively.

14. I declare that my prayers are like arrows piercing the hearts of principalities, weakening their hold.

15. By the power of the Holy Spirit, I release healing and restoration upon areas affected by principalities' oppression.

16. I proclaim that the angels of God encamp around me and my loved ones, providing divine protection.

17. I bind any spirit of division and disunity that principalities may attempt to sow among believers.

18. I loose a spirit of unity, love, and cooperation among God's people as we stand together in prayer.

19. In the name of Jesus, I command every principality to relinquish its grip over governments, institutions, and individuals.

20. I declare that God's will shall prevail, and His kingdom shall advance in every sphere of influence.

21. By the authority of Jesus Christ, I break every curse, hex, and spell released by principalities.

22. I release the blood of Jesus as a shield, protecting me and my loved ones from all harm and evil.

23. I declare that my mind is renewed by the Word of God, making me resistant to the lies and deceptions of principalities.

24. I bind every spirit of addiction, oppression, and depression in Jesus' name.

25. I loose the spirit of freedom, joy, and peace upon those who have been oppressed by principalities.

26. In the name of Jesus, I command the release of those held captive by the influence of principalities.

27. I declare that every demonic network and communication among principalities is disrupted and dismantled.

28. I loose the angels of God to wage war on my behalf and to carry out God's divine assignments.

29. I decree that I am an overcomer in Christ, and no principality can stand against the authority of Jesus' name.

30. In the name of Jesus, I plead the blood of Christ over my home, my family, and my community.

31. I declare that the power of prayer and intercession is a mighty weapon against principalities.

32. By the authority of Jesus, I bind any spirit of hopelessness and despair that principalities may try to release.

33. I loose the spirit of faith, hope, and expectancy, knowing that God is greater than any principality.

34. In Jesus' name, I declare that the plans of principalities are exposed and brought into the light.

35. I decree that God's truth prevails, and every lie of the enemy is exposed and defeated.

36. I bind every spirit of pride and arrogance that fuels the influence of principalities.

37. I loose a spirit of humility and contrition, inviting God's grace and mercy to flow.

38. In the name of Jesus, I declare that every principality is subject to the authority of the cross.

39. I release the power of forgiveness, knowing that it breaks the chains that principalities seek to forge.

40. I stand firm in the victory of Christ, declaring that no principality can withstand the might and authority of our Lord and Savior. Amen!

Chapter 11

The Midnight Roar:
Releasing Your Battle Cry

In the darkest of hours, when the world is shrouded in silence and the veil between the natural and supernatural realms is at its thinnest, the midnight hour becomes a sacred battleground. It is during this time that the Midnight Warriors awaken, armed not with conventional weapons but with the power of their voices—their battle cries.

In the realm of spiritual warfare, the concept of the battle cry carries profound significance. It represents a clarion call to the heavens and a declaration of war against the forces of darkness. It is a manifestation of faith, a vocalization of authority, and a conduit through which the supernatural intersects with the natural. In this chapter, we delve deep into the significance of the Midnight Roar, exploring its biblical foundations, its practical applications, and its transformative power in the life of a warrior.

The Biblical Foundation of the Midnight Roar

The Midnight Roar finds its roots in the ancient scriptures, where it is often depicted as the voice of God Himself or His chosen warriors shaking the heavens and the earth with their declarations. Let's explore some key biblical references:

1. The Shout at Jericho: One of the most iconic instances of the battle cry in the Bible occurred during the conquest of Jericho. The Israelites, led by Joshua, were instructed to march around the city in silence for six days. On the seventh day, they were commanded to shout a great battle cry. The walls of Jericho crumbled, and victory was achieved (Joshua 6:1-20).

2. David's Battle Cry: The Psalms are filled with Davidic declarations that can be likened to battle cries. In Psalm 18:6, David proclaimed, "In my distress, I called to the Lord; I cried to my God for help. From His temple, He heard my voice; my cry came before Him, into His ears." David's cries were not merely words but expressions of his heart's faith in God's deliverance.

3. Paul and Silas in Prison: In Acts 16, we find Paul and Silas imprisoned in Philippi. Instead of succumbing to despair, they prayed and sang hymns to God. Their midnight worship became a supernatural battle cry that not only broke their chains but also led to the salvation of their jailer and his household.

The Midnight Roar in Practice

The Midnight Roar is not a mere shouting of words into the darkness. It is a strategic act of spiritual warfare, and like any effective strategy, it requires intentionality and understanding. Here's how you can practically apply the Midnight Roar in your spiritual battles:

1. Alignment with God's Word: Your battle cry should always align with the Word of God. This alignment ensures that you are speaking God's truth and not merely uttering empty words. Study the Bible, find relevant passages, and incorporate them into your declarations.

2. Confidence in Your Authority: As a believer in Christ, you have been given authority over the powers of darkness (Luke 10:19). Your battle cry should reflect this confidence in your spiritual authority. Declare your authority in Christ and command the enemy to flee.

3. Worship and Praise: The Midnight Roar often begins with worship and praise. Singing hymns and songs of praise not only uplift your spirit but also create an atmosphere where the presence of God can manifest powerfully.

4. Specific Declarations: Be specific in your declarations. Identify the areas of your life or the situations you are praying about. For example, if you are battling sickness, declare healing scriptures. If you are in financial distress, declare God's provision.

5. Persistence: Just as the Israelites marched around Jericho for seven days, be persistent in your midnight prayers and declarations. Sometimes breakthroughs come after consistent and prolonged spiritual warfare.

6. Unity in Prayer: If possible, join with other believers in your midnight prayers. There is power in unity, and the collective Midnight Roar of warriors can shake the spiritual realm.

The Transformative Power of the Midnight Roar

The Midnight Roar is not just a ritual; it is a transformational experience. As you consistently release your battle cry in the midnight hour, several profound changes occur:

1. Spiritual Sensitivity: Your spiritual senses become sharpened. You become more attuned to the presence of God and the strategies of the enemy.

2. Increased Faith: The Midnight Roar strengthens your faith as you see the tangible results of your declarations. You develop unwavering confidence in God's power.

3. Victory and Breakthrough: Chains are broken, walls crumble, and strongholds are demolished. The Midnight Roar paves the way for victory and breakthrough in every area of your life.

4. Prophetic Revelation: In the midnight silence, God often releases prophetic revelation and guidance. You receive insight into His plans and purposes for your life.

5. Empowerment of Others: Your Midnight Roar not only impacts your life but also empowers those around you. It inspires others to rise as warriors in the kingdom of God.

The Midnight Roar is a potent weapon in the arsenal of a spiritual warrior. It is a divine invitation to partner with God in disrupting the activities of the powers of darkness. As you release your battle cry with faith, authority, and persistence, you will experience transformation, victory, and a deeper intimacy with the Almighty. The midnight hour is not a time of fear but a time of power, and the Midnight Roar is your key to unlocking that power. So, let your voice rise, let your faith soar, and let the darkness tremble at the sound of your Midnight Roar.

Warfare Prayer

1. In the mighty name of Jesus, I declare that the Midnight Roar is my divine birthright, and I will use it to overcome the powers of darkness.

2. I take authority over every demonic force that opposes my life, my family, and my destiny. In Jesus' name, I command them to flee.

3. By the power of the blood of Jesus, I nullify every curse, hex, or spell that has been spoken against me. They have no power over me.

4. I declare that my battle cry is a sound of victory. It shatters the plans of the enemy and releases the presence of God.

5. In the name of Jesus, I rebuke fear, doubt, and unbelief. I am filled with faith, confidence, and unwavering trust in God.

6. Every stronghold in my life is demolished by the authority of Jesus' name. I am free from bondage and oppression.

7. I release the fire of the Holy Spirit in my prayers. It consumes every work of darkness and purifies my life.

8. I declare that I am a worshipper of the Most High God. My praises are a weapon that confounds the enemy.

9. I take authority over sickness and infirmity. In Jesus' name, I declare divine healing and restoration over my body.

10. I declare that my declarations are in alignment with God's Word. His promises are my foundation, and I stand on them with confidence.

11. Every demonic assignment against my family is canceled. I declare a hedge of protection around my loved ones.

12. I release the angels of God to encamp around me and go before me in battle. They are mighty warriors on my behalf.

13. In the name of Jesus, I command every storm in my life to be still. Peace and tranquility reign in my circumstances.

14. I declare that I am a victor, not a victim. I overcome every trial and tribulation through the power of Jesus' name.

15. I release supernatural dreams and visions. I receive divine guidance and insight from the Lord.

16. I take authority over financial lack and declare that God is my provider. His abundance flows into my life.

17. I rebuke every spirit of depression and anxiety. I am filled with the joy of the Lord, which is my strength.

18. I declare that my words have creative power. I speak life, blessing, and favor over every situation.

19. In Jesus' name, I bind the spirit of division and strife. Unity and love prevail in my relationships.

20. I declare that I am more than a conqueror through Christ who strengthens me. No weapon formed against me shall prosper.

21. I take authority over generational curses and declare that my bloodline is cleansed by the blood of Jesus.

22. I release the sound of revival in my community. Souls are saved, and hearts are turned toward God.

23. I declare that I am a vessel of honor for God's purposes. I am used mightily in His kingdom.

24. In the name of Jesus, I command doors of opportunity to open, and every hindrance to my progress is removed.

25. I rebuke the spirit of fear that tries to paralyze me. I walk in boldness and courage.

26. I release forgiveness and choose to let go of past offenses. I am free from bitterness and resentment.

27. I declare that I am an overcomer by the blood of the Lamb and the word of my testimony.

28. In Jesus' name, I bind the forces of darkness that seek to steal, kill, and destroy. They have no power here.

29. I release divine favor and divine connections into my life. God orders my steps.

30. I take authority over every storm in my marriage and family life. Peace and harmony reign.

31. I declare that I am a warrior of light. Darkness flees in my presence.

32. In the name of Jesus, I bind the spirit of lack and poverty. I walk in prosperity and abundance.

33. I rebuke every attack on my mind and emotions. I have the mind of Christ and experience His peace.

34. I release supernatural wisdom and discernment. I make sound decisions guided by the Holy Spirit.

35. I declare that I am an instrument of revival in my generation. God's glory shines through me.

36. In Jesus' name, I bind every hindering spirit that opposes the fulfillment of God's promises in my life.

37. I release the love of God to flow through me, touching lives and transforming hearts.

38. I take authority over every addiction and declare freedom and deliverance in Jesus' name.

39. I declare that my prayers are powerful and effective. They bring about change in the spiritual realm.

40. I release the Midnight Roar with boldness and faith. Every obstacle is removed, and every mountain is cast into the sea.

Chapter 12

Warrior's Worship:
Songs of Victory in the Night

In the darkest hours of the night, when the world sleeps and the powers of darkness prowl, there exists a secret weapon that the midnight warriors wield—a weapon so potent that it can shatter the very foundations of evil. This weapon is not forged in steel, nor is it a product of human craftsmanship. It is the weapon of worship, a spiritual symphony that resonates in the heavenly realms and strikes terror into the hearts of the enemy.

The Midnight Symphony

Picture this: You stand in the midst of the battlefield of the mind, surrounded by the shadows of doubt, fear, and despair. The enemy's whispers grow louder, his forces closing in. But you are not defenseless. You lift your voice, not in fear, but in worship. The melody that escapes your lips is not just a song; it is a declaration of victory. It is a symphony of faith.

Midnight worship is not your typical Sunday morning hymn-singing. It is a battle cry set to music. It is the defiant anthem of a warrior who knows that the battle belongs to the Lord. When you engage in midnight worship, you are not merely singing songs; you are releasing the supernatural power of God into the spiritual battleground.

The Heart of Worship

To understand the potency of midnight worship, we must first grasp its essence. Worship is not a performance; it is a posture of the heart. It is an act of surrender, an acknowledgment of God's supreme authority, and a declaration of His goodness and faithfulness.

In the dark of night, as you lift your voice and your hands, you are saying, "I trust You, Lord, even when I cannot see the way. I believe in Your promises, even in the midst of adversity." Your worship becomes a fragrant offering before the throne of God, a sweet aroma that dispels the stench of the enemy's schemes.

Songs of Deliverance

The Bible is filled with accounts of the power of worship in the face of adversity. In 2 Chronicles 20, we find the story of Jehoshaphat, a king facing an overwhelming enemy alliance. His response? He appointed singers to go ahead of the army, praising the beauty of holiness. As they sang, the Lord set ambushes against the enemy, and they were defeated.

Likewise, when Paul and Silas found themselves imprisoned in Acts 16, they didn't wallow in despair. In the darkest hour of the night, they began to sing hymns of praise to God. Their worship shook the foundations of the prison, and the doors swung open. Midnight worship brought their deliverance.

Weapons of Melody

Midnight worship is not confined to a specific musical genre or style. It transcends culture and tradition. Whether you prefer contemporary Christian songs, gospel, hymns, or spontaneous melodies birthed in the moment, what matters is the heart behind the worship.

Each note, each lyric, becomes a spiritual weapon in your hands. The words you sing are not mere lyrics; they are decrees and declarations of God's power and authority. As you sing of His faithfulness, you remind the enemy of his defeat. As you declare His goodness, you proclaim that darkness cannot prevail in the presence of the Light.

The Dance of Victory

Worship is not limited to the vocal expression of praise. It extends to the movement of your body. In the midnight hour, consider the dance of David before the Ark of the Covenant. He leaped and twirled with abandon, his worship an uncontainable outpouring of joy and gratitude.

In the same way, your midnight worship can include dance. It is a physical manifestation of your spiritual victory. As you move in rhythm with the music, you are declaring that the chains of oppression are broken, and you are free in Christ. Your dance is a testimony to the world that you serve a living and victorious God.

The Symphony of Unity

There is a unique power in corporate midnight worship. When midnight warriors gather in unity, their worship becomes a symphony that shakes the heavens. In Acts 12, the church gathered to pray for Peter, who was imprisoned. As they prayed, an angel was sent to rescue him. Their collective prayers and worship created a supernatural intervention.

In the midnight hours, consider joining with fellow warriors to worship. Whether in a physical gathering or a virtual one, when voices rise in harmony and hearts unite in worship, the enemy's plans crumble. Unity in worship amplifies its impact.

Decrees and Declarations

Midnight worship is not merely singing songs; it is releasing decrees and declarations that shift the spiritual atmosphere. As you worship, proclaim the promises of God. Declare that you are more than a conqueror through Christ. Decree that the enemy's plans are thwarted, and you walk in victory.

Your declarations become a spiritual battering ram against the enemy's gates. As you lift your voice, declare:

- "I am a child of the Most High God, and no weapon formed against me shall prosper."
- "The Lord is my light and my salvation; whom shall I fear?"
- "Greater is He who is in me than he who is in the world."

These declarations, rooted in Scripture, become arrows in your quiver, ready to pierce the darkness.

A Lifestyle of Worship

Midnight worship should not be confined to specific moments of crisis. It is a lifestyle—a continual posture of the heart. When you make worship a daily habit, you cultivate an atmosphere of victory around you.

Begin and end your day in worship. Sing in the shower, praise in the kitchen, and adore in the car. Let your life become a melody that never ceases. As you do, you will find that the powers of darkness dare not approach the one who is continually enveloped in the presence of God.

In the darkest moments of the night, when the powers of darkness seek to intimidate and oppress, the midnight warrior takes up the weapon of worship. This chapter has explored the profound impact of worship in spiritual warfare. It is not a passive act but a powerful declaration of faith and victory.

Remember, in the midnight hour, you are not alone. The God of angel armies stands with you. Lift your voice, declare His goodness, and dance in the face of adversity. Let your worship be a symphony of victory that echoes through the heavens, disrupting the activities of darkness and ushering in the light of God's presence.

As you make worship a lifestyle, you will discover that you are not just a warrior; you are a worshipper-warrior—an unstoppable force in the kingdom of God. Embrace this truth, and watch as the powers of darkness crumble before you.

Warfare Prayer

1. In the mighty name of Jesus, I declare that I am a midnight warrior, armed with the weapon of worship, ready to confront the powers of darkness.

2. By the blood of Jesus, I break every chain of fear and doubt that hinders my worship in the midnight hour.

3. I decree that my worship is a symphony of faith that resonates in the heavenly realms, striking terror into the hearts of the enemy.

4. In the name of Jesus, I release the supernatural power of God through my midnight worship, shattering the foundations of evil.

5. I declare that my worship is not a performance but a posture of the heart, an act of surrender to the Almighty God.

6. By the authority of Jesus, I acknowledge God's supreme authority over every situation in my life and declare His goodness and faithfulness.

7. I decree that my worship dispels the stench of the enemy's schemes and fills the atmosphere with the fragrance of God's presence.

8. In Jesus' name, I stand on 2 Chronicles 20 and declare that as I worship, God sets ambushes against my enemies, and they are defeated.

9. I declare that my worship breaks the chains of oppression, and I walk in the freedom that Christ has secured for me.

10. By the blood of Jesus, I declare that my worship releases a supernatural intervention in times of crisis, just as in Acts 12.

11. I decree that my worship is a symphony of unity when I gather with fellow warriors, amplifying its impact and shaking the heavens.

12. In the name of Jesus, I release decrees and declarations in my worship, shifting the spiritual atmosphere and thwarting the enemy's plans.

13. I declare that I am more than a conqueror through Christ, and no weapon formed against me shall prosper.

14. By the authority of Jesus, I proclaim that the Lord is my light and my salvation; I shall fear no evil.

15. I decree that greater is He who is in me than he who is in the world, and I walk in victory.

16. In Jesus' name, I make worship a daily habit, cultivating an atmosphere of victory around me.

17. I declare that I begin and end my day in worship, and my life is a continual melody that never ceases.

18. By the blood of Jesus, I decree that in the midnight hour, the God of angel armies stands with me, and I am enveloped in His presence.

19. I declare that I am a worshipper-warrior, an unstoppable force in the kingdom of God, and darkness dare not approach me.

20. In the name of Jesus, I release the power of worship to disrupt the activities of darkness and usher in the light of God's presence.

21. I decree that as I lift my voice, the enemy's plans crumble, and the powers of darkness flee.

22. By the authority of Jesus, I declare that my worship is a declaration of victory, and I am a conqueror in Christ.

23. I proclaim that my worship is a fragrant offering before the throne of God, pleasing to His ears.

24. In Jesus' name, I release the dance of victory, declaring that I am free in Christ and chains are broken.

25. I declare that my worship is not confined to specific moments but is a lifestyle that cultivates an atmosphere of triumph.

26. By the blood of Jesus, I decree that I am surrounded by the presence of God, and no darkness can prevail in His light.

27. I declare that I am a worshipper-warrior, standing boldly in the face of adversity, knowing that the battle belongs to the Lord.

28. In the name of Jesus, I release the power of worship to shake the heavens and disrupt the enemy's strategies.

29. I decree that as I worship, I am reminded of God's promises, and fear and doubt have no place in my life.

30. By the authority of Jesus, I declare that I am a part of the midnight symphony, a spiritual symphony that terrifies the enemy.

31. I proclaim that my worship is a symphony of faith that shatters the foundations of evil and releases God's power.

32. In Jesus' name, I release decrees and declarations that shift the spiritual atmosphere and bring forth God's victory.

33. I declare that my worship is not just a song; it is a declaration of God's goodness and faithfulness.

34. By the blood of Jesus, I decree that my worship is a weapon that pierces the darkness and dispels the enemy's schemes.

35. I declare that I am a worshipper-warrior, and my worship is a fragrance that overcomes the stench of the enemy.

36. In the name of Jesus, I release the dance of David, leaping and twirling with joy and gratitude, declaring my victory in Christ.

37. I decree that my worship is a lifestyle, a continual posture of the heart that cultivates an atmosphere of triumph.

38. By the authority of Jesus, I declare that my worship is a symphony of unity when I gather with fellow warriors, shaking the heavens.

39. I proclaim that my worship releases a supernatural intervention, just as in Acts 12, and God's deliverance comes swiftly.

40. In Jesus' name, I declare that as I lift my voice and release decrees in worship, I am an unstoppable force for God's kingdom, and the enemy trembles in my presence.

Chapter 13

The Midnight Intercessors:
Praying for the Nations

In the darkest hour of the night, when the world is shrouded in stillness, a cadre of spiritual warriors emerges from the shadows. They are the Midnight Intercessors, vigilant sentinels in the spiritual realm, engaged in a battle that transcends time and space. Their mission: to pray for the nations with a fervor that shakes the heavens and shifts the course of history. In this chapter, we delve into the profound significance of midnight intercession, exploring its power, purpose, and the strategies that make it a force to be reckoned with.

The Midnight Hour: A Gateway to the Supernatural

Midnight holds a unique place in the realm of spiritual warfare. It is the time when the veil between the natural and supernatural is at its thinnest, a time when the forces of darkness are most active, and a time when the cries of God's people can pierce the heavens with unprecedented clarity.

The Biblical Foundation: Midnight intercession has deep biblical roots. In the book of Acts, we find the account of Paul and Silas praying and singing hymns at midnight in a Philippian prison. Their prayers shook the foundations of the prison, resulting in not only their own liberation but also the salvation of their jailer and his household (Acts 16:25-34). This serves as a powerful testament to the impact of midnight prayers and intercession.

A Global Perspective: The call to pray for the nations is not limited by borders or geography. As Midnight Intercessors, we are tasked with lifting up the nations of the world before the throne of God. It is a divine mandate to seek the welfare of every people group, to intercede for their salvation, healing, and restoration.

Strategies of Midnight Intercession

1. Identification and Repentance

Before interceding for the nations, we must first identify with their struggles and sins. Just as Daniel identified with the sins of Israel when he prayed in Babylon, we should carry the burden of the nations' transgressions on our hearts. Midnight intercessors understand that repentance is a powerful key to unlocking God's mercy and intervention.

2. Praying in Tongues

The gift of speaking in tongues is a valuable tool in midnight intercession. When we pray in tongues, we bypass our limited understanding and allow the Holy Spirit to pray through us according to God's perfect will (Romans

8:26-27). This is especially crucial when praying for nations with complex issues and languages.

3. Prophetic Declarations

Midnight intercessors are called to release prophetic declarations over nations. These declarations are rooted in God's promises and are spoken with unwavering faith. Prophetic decrees have the power to shift spiritual atmospheres and align nations with God's purposes.

4. Travailing Prayer

Midnight intercession often involves travailing prayer, where we earnestly labor in prayer as if giving birth to God's purposes for the nations (Galatians 4:19). This type of prayer requires spiritual stamina and a willingness to persevere in the face of opposition.

Engaging in Spiritual Warfare

Midnight intercessors are not passive observers but active participants in spiritual warfare. They engage in battle with the enemy's forces that seek to hinder the destiny of nations. This battle is not against flesh and blood but against principalities, powers, and spiritual forces of wickedness (Ephesians 6:12).

Binding and Loosing: Midnight intercessors understand the authority given to them by Christ to bind the forces of darkness and to loose the blessings and purposes of God. This is a strategic aspect of spiritual warfare that can have a profound impact on nations.

Standing in the Gap: Just as Abraham interceded for Sodom and Gomorrah, midnight intercessors stand in the gap for nations that are in moral and spiritual decline. They plead for God's mercy and grace to spare these nations from judgment.

Global Impact

The prayers of midnight intercessors have a ripple effect that transcends borders. As we pray for the nations, we become conduits of God's love, mercy, and power. Nations are transformed, leaders are guided by divine wisdom, and revival sweeps across continents.

Historical Examples: Throughout history, we see the impact of intercessors who prayed for nations. From the prayers of missionaries who brought the gospel to unreached peoples to the prayers of believers who stood against tyranny and injustice, the influence of midnight intercession is undeniable.

The Great Commission: Midnight intercession aligns with the Great Commission given by Jesus to make disciples of all nations (Matthew 28:19-20). When we pray for the nations, we participate in the fulfillment of this commission, paving the way for the gospel to reach the ends of the earth.

Midnight intercession is not for the faint of heart. It requires a deep commitment to prayer, a willingness to wrestle in the spiritual realm, and an unwavering faith in God's power to transform nations. As Midnight Warriors, we have been called to this sacred task, and in doing so, we partner with the Creator of the universe to bring about His divine purposes on a global scale.

In the stillness of the midnight hour, let us rise as intercessors, armed with prayer and faith, to pray for the nations and see the powers of darkness tremble before the might of our God. It is in these moments of communion with the Most High that we truly become warriors in the midnight, shaping the course of nations and ushering in the kingdom of heaven on earth.

Warfare Prayer

1. In the name of Jesus, I declare that as a Midnight Intercessor, I am a vessel of God's love and light, shining in the darkest places of the world.

2. By the authority of Jesus Christ, I bind every stronghold and principality that hinders the nations from knowing God's truth and salvation.

3. I decree that the hearts of leaders in every nation are turned towards righteousness and justice, guided by divine wisdom.

4. In Jesus' name, I break the chains of corruption and oppression that bind nations, releasing the captives to freedom.

5. I declare that the gospel of Jesus Christ will penetrate every corner of the earth, bringing salvation, healing, and transformation.

6. By the power of the Holy Spirit, I pray for revival to sweep across nations, igniting a hunger for God's presence and truth.

7. I decree that every plan of the enemy to sow division and discord among nations is thwarted by the unity of the Spirit.

8. In the name of Jesus, I plead for God's mercy over nations facing natural disasters, economic crises, and political turmoil.

9. I declare that the voice of the oppressed is heard, and justice prevails in nations plagued by injustice.

10. By the authority of Christ, I release angels to encamp around the leaders of nations, guarding them against evil influences.

11. I decree that the nations will turn to the one true God, renouncing false gods and idols.

12. In Jesus' name, I speak peace over regions torn apart by conflict and war, and I declare an end to violence.

13. I declare that the light of God's Word shines brightly, dispelling spiritual darkness in every nation.

14. By the power of the cross, I break generational curses and strongholds that have plagued nations for centuries.

15. I decree that the church rises up as a beacon of hope, love, and compassion in every nation.

16. In the name of Jesus, I pray for the healing of land and people in nations affected by environmental disasters and diseases.

17. I declare that the hearts of citizens are turned towards God, and they seek Him with all their strength.

18. By the authority of Christ, I release supernatural provisions and resources for nations in times of need.

19. I decree that the hearts of children and youth in every nation are protected and guided in the ways of the Lord.

20. In Jesus' name, I declare that the power of addiction is broken, and deliverance sweeps across nations.

21. I declare that the enemy's plans to silence the voice of the church in nations are utterly defeated.

22. By the power of the Holy Spirit, I release a spirit of repentance and revival in the hearts of the people.

23. I decree that God's glory is manifested in signs, wonders, and miracles in nations.

24. In the name of Jesus, I bind the spirits of terrorism and extremism, and I decree peace and security.

25. I declare that the nations will honor and protect the sanctity of life from conception to natural death.

26. By the authority of Christ, I pray for unity and reconciliation among divided nations and peoples.

27. I decree that the educational systems in nations are infused with godly wisdom and values.

28. In Jesus' name, I break the power of human trafficking and exploitation, setting captives free.

29. I declare that the nations will seek God's guidance in their policies and decisions.

30. By the power of the cross, I declare an end to religious persecution and the free practice of faith.

31. I decree that the Church rises as a unifying force, breaking down racial and ethnic barriers in nations.

32. In the name of Jesus, I bind the spirits of poverty and lack, releasing economic prosperity.

33. I declare that the nations will become centers of compassion, caring for the orphaned, widowed, and vulnerable.

34. By the authority of Christ, I pray for the healing of deep wounds and historical injustices in nations.

35. I decree that the nations will be known for their generosity and willingness to aid those in need.

36. In Jesus' name, I declare that every plot and scheme of the enemy against nations is exposed and nullified.

37. I release a spirit of reconciliation and forgiveness among divided communities and nations.

38. By the power of the Holy Spirit, I pray for an outpouring of love and compassion in the hearts of leaders.

39. I decree that the nations will become centers of worship, exalting the name of Jesus.

40. In the name of Jesus, I speak blessings and divine favor over every nation, for God's glory and purposes to be fulfilled.

Chapter 14

Angels on Assignment:
Partners in Midnight Warfare

In the depths of the midnight hour, when the world is shrouded in darkness and the forces of evil seem to be at their strongest, there is a divine alliance that comes to the aid of the Midnight Warrior. These celestial beings, radiant and powerful, are none other than the angels of God. In this chapter, we will delve deep into the mysterious realm of angels and explore their role as our partners in the fierce battle of midnight warfare.

Unveiling the Angelic Host

To comprehend the significance of angels in our spiritual warfare, we must first acknowledge their existence and purpose. Angels are not mere mythological entities or the stuff of fairy tales; they are real, tangible beings created by God to serve His divine purposes. The Bible is replete with references to these heavenly messengers, and their appearances range from the Old Testament to the New.

One cannot ignore the fact that the midnight hour holds a unique spiritual significance. It is a time when the veil between the earthly realm and the heavenly realm grows thin, allowing for increased angelic activity.

Midnight is when our prayers, laden with fervor and faith, reach the ears of God, and it is also when angels are dispatched to carry out His will on our behalf.

The Ministry of Midnight Angels

Angels play multifaceted roles in the realm of midnight warfare. They are not passive observers but active participants in the battle against the powers of darkness. Understanding their ministries is crucial for every Midnight Warrior:

1. Messengers of Revelation: Angels often bring divine revelations and insights to those engaged in midnight warfare. They deliver messages from the throne of God, providing strategic guidance and direction.

2. Guardians of Protection: Angels serve as our spiritual bodyguards, encamping around us to shield us from harm. They create a hedge of protection, deflecting the fiery darts of the enemy.

3. Warrior Angels: Some angels are specifically assigned to engage in combat against demonic forces. They wage war in the spiritual realm, battling principalities and powers on our behalf.

4. Ministers of Healing: Angels carry the healing balm of God's presence. In the midnight hour, they are dispatched to minister to those who are sick or suffering, bringing comfort and restoration.

5. Agents of Deliverance: When we cry out in the midnight hour for deliverance from bondage, angels come as liberators. They break chains, unlock prison doors, and set the captives free.

The Partnership: How Angels Respond to Prayer

Our partnership with angels in midnight warfare is not a one-sided affair. It is a divine synergy that operates through prayer, faith, and obedience. When we align our prayers with God's will, angels respond with power and precision.

1. Prayer Activation: Angels are activated by our prayers. The more fervent and faith-filled our prayers are, the more angels are dispatched to our aid. It is as if they await our call to action.

2. Spiritual Weapons: Angels wield spiritual weapons that are far superior to any earthly arsenal. They carry swords of light and shields of faith. When we engage in spiritual warfare, they fight alongside us, reinforcing our efforts.

3. Binding and Loosing: Angels assist in binding the forces of darkness and loosing the blessings and favor of God. As we decree and declare in the midnight hour, angels enforce these decrees in the spiritual realm.

4. Worship and Praise: Angels are drawn to worship and praise. When we lift our voices in adoration during midnight worship, it releases a heavenly atmosphere where angels thrive.

Guarding Your Midnight Hour

While angels are powerful allies, it is important to remember that they respond to the authority of God's Word and the leading of the Holy Spirit. Here are some key principles for partnering effectively with angels in your midnight warfare:

1. Stay Aligned with God: Ensure that your prayers are aligned with God's will and His Word. Angels hearken to His commands, so our prayers must reflect His heart.

2. Walk in Holiness: The presence of angels is attracted to purity and holiness. Live a life of righteousness to maintain a strong connection with the angelic realm.

3. Decree with Authority: As Midnight Warriors, we have been given authority by Christ. Use that authority to decree and declare God's promises in your midnight prayers.

4. Acknowledge Their Presence: In your midnight warfare, acknowledge the presence of angels. Thank God for their assistance and partnership.

Embracing the Angelic Dimension

In the dark and turbulent battlefield of midnight warfare, angels are our divine partners, fighting alongside us with heavenly might and supernatural power. Their role is not passive; it is active, engaged, and responsive to our prayers and declarations. As we embrace the angelic dimension of spiritual warfare, we tap into a wellspring of divine support that empowers us to overcome the powers of darkness and disrupt their activities.

Remember, you are never alone in your midnight battles. Angels stand ready, awaiting your call to action. Embrace this partnership, walk in faith, and watch as the powers of darkness tremble at the presence of these heavenly warriors. With angels as your partners, you are truly a Midnight Warrior, equipped to prevail in the darkest of hours.

Warfare Prayer

1. In the mighty name of Jesus, I declare that angels are my partners in midnight warfare, ready to respond to my prayers.

2. I decree that the angelic host surrounds me, creating an impenetrable fortress of protection.

3. By the authority of Jesus Christ, I activate the ministry of angels to bring divine revelations and insights into my life.

4. I declare that angels are waging war on my behalf against every demonic force that seeks to harm me or hinder God's purpose for my life.

5. I bind and rebuke every spirit of darkness in Jesus' name, knowing that angels are enforcing this binding.

6. I release the angels of healing to minister to my body, soul, and spirit, bringing restoration and wholeness.

7. By the power of the Holy Spirit, I call forth angels as agents of deliverance, breaking every chain and setting me free from bondage.

8. I decree that my prayers activate the angels of God, and they are dispatched with speed and precision.

9. I release the angels to wield their spiritual weapons on my behalf, defeating every adversary in the heavenly realms.

10. I declare that my prayers are in alignment with God's will, and angels are carrying out His divine plans in my life.

11. By the authority of Jesus, I command angels to stand guard over my midnight hour, ensuring that it is a time of spiritual victory and breakthrough.

12. I declare that angels respond to my prayers with joy and readiness, for they are eager to fulfill God's purposes.

13. I release the angels to bind the forces of darkness that oppose God's blessings in my life.

14. I take authority over any spiritual opposition and decree that angels are releasing breakthroughs and blessings.

15. I decree that angels encamp around my loved ones, protecting them from harm and danger.

16. By faith, I declare that angels are enforcing God's divine order and justice in my circumstances.

17. I release the angels to minister to those who are sick or in need, bringing comfort and healing in Jesus' name.

18. I declare that my life is a magnet for angelic activity, and I welcome their presence.

19. I take authority over any spiritual strongholds in my life, knowing that angels are demolishing them.

20. I decree that angels are assisting me in my worship and praise, creating an atmosphere where God's presence is manifested.

21. I release angels to guard my dreams and visions, ensuring they are in alignment with God's purposes.

22. I declare that angels are releasing supernatural wisdom and understanding into my life.

23. By the power of Jesus' name, I command angels to fight against every spiritual adversary that seeks to hinder my progress.

24. I release the angels to bring divine favor and blessings into every area of my life.

25. I decree that angels are agents of peace, and they are bringing peace to every storm in my life.

26. I declare that angels are lifting me up in times of weakness, giving me strength and courage.

27. By faith, I call forth the angels to break every chain of addiction and bondage in my life.

28. I release the angels to minister to the needs of the nations, bringing healing and transformation.

29. I declare that angels are releasing signs and wonders in response to my prayers.

30. I take authority over every demonic assignment against my family and decree that angels are thwarting them.

31. I release angels to surround my home, creating an atmosphere of divine protection and peace.

32. I decree that angels are on assignment to bring breakthroughs and prosperity into my life.

33. By the blood of Jesus, I command angels to cleanse and purify my spiritual environment.

34. I release the angels to guard my thoughts and emotions, bringing peace and clarity.

35. I declare that angels are carrying out God's plans and purposes for my life with precision and accuracy.

36. I take authority over any spirit of fear and anxiety and decree that angels are replacing them with God's peace.

37. I release the angels to bring divine connections and relationships into my life.

38. I decree that angels are releasing divine protection over my finances and resources.

39. By faith, I declare that angels are at work in my family, bringing unity and love.

40. I release angels to minister to the lonely and brokenhearted, bringing comfort and healing in Jesus' name.

Chapter 15

Smashing Strongholds:
Breaking the Enemy's Grip

In the spiritual realm, strongholds are like fortresses that the enemy builds within our minds and hearts, strategically designed to keep us captive and hinder our walk with God. These strongholds can take many forms, including addictive behaviors, negative thought patterns, and deeply ingrained sinful habits. In this chapter, we will delve into the powerful methods and spiritual weapons required to identify, confront, and ultimately demolish these strongholds, allowing us to experience true freedom and victory in Christ.

Understanding Strongholds

Before we can effectively smash strongholds, we must first understand what they are and how they operate. Strongholds are often built upon lies and deception. The enemy feeds us false beliefs about ourselves, God, and the world around us. These lies take root in our minds and become the foundation of the stronghold. Over time, they solidify and gain control over our thoughts, emotions, and actions.

For instance, someone struggling with addiction may believe the lie that they are powerless to change. This belief becomes a stronghold, keeping them trapped in destructive behavior. Another person might have a stronghold of bitterness, holding onto grudges and unforgiveness, which poisons their relationships and hinders their spiritual growth.

Strongholds are like chains that bind us, limiting our potential and obstructing our relationship with God. They are not limited to individuals; they can also affect families, churches, and entire communities. Recognizing the presence of strongholds is the first step in smashing them.

The Weapons of Our Warfare

The Bible tells us that our weapons in spiritual warfare are not of this world (2 Corinthians 10:4). They are divinely powerful and capable of pulling down strongholds. Here are some of the key weapons in our arsenal:

1. The Word of God

The Word of God is our sword (Ephesians 6:17). It is sharp and powerful, able to pierce through the lies that form strongholds. To use this weapon effectively, we must immerse ourselves in Scripture, meditating on it day and night (Joshua 1:8). By doing so, we replace the enemy's lies with God's truth.

2. Prayer and Fasting

Prayer and fasting are mighty tools for smashing strongholds. When we pray fervently and seek God's face, we invite His presence and power into our lives. Fasting, when done with a humble heart, can break the chains of addiction and release us from the grip of the enemy.

3. Repentance and Confession

Acknowledging our sins and confessing them before God is essential. The enemy often uses hidden sin as a foundation for strongholds. Confession brings those sins into the light, where they lose their power.

4. Worship and Praise

Praising God in the midst of our struggles is a powerful act of spiritual warfare. It shifts our focus from the stronghold to the Almighty God who can demolish it. Worship and praise invite the presence of God, and where His presence is, strongholds cannot stand.

5. Community and Accountability

We are not meant to fight this battle alone. Surrounding ourselves with a community of believers who can provide support, encouragement, and accountability is crucial. Sharing our struggles and victories with others can weaken the grip of strongholds.

Strategies for Smashing Strongholds

Now that we understand the weapons at our disposal, let's explore some practical strategies for smashing strongholds:

1. Identify the Stronghold

The first step is to identify the specific stronghold you are dealing with. Is it an addiction, a negative thought pattern, or a sinful behavior? Be specific and honest with yourself.

2. Renew Your Mind

Once you've identified the stronghold, renew your mind with God's Word. Replace the enemy's lies with God's truth. Memorize and meditate on Scripture that directly addresses your struggle.

3. Prayer and Fasting

Engage in focused, persistent prayer. Cry out to God for deliverance and healing. Consider fasting as a way to intensify your prayers and demonstrate your desperation for breakthrough.

4. Accountability and Support

Seek out a trusted friend, pastor, or counselor who can provide accountability and support. Confide in someone who will pray with you and help you stay on the path to freedom.

5. Stay Persistent

Breaking strongholds can be a battle, and the enemy may not give up easily. Stay persistent in your efforts. Even if you experience setbacks, don't lose hope. Keep using your spiritual weapons and pressing forward.

6. Declare Your Victory

Finally, declare your victory in Christ. Speak out loud that the stronghold has no power over you because you are a child of God. Continue to worship and praise God, even in the midst of the battle.

Smashing strongholds is not a one-time event but an ongoing process. It requires determination, faith, and a deep reliance on God's power. As midnight warriors, we have been equipped with the authority and weapons to break free from the enemy's grip. By understanding strongholds, using our spiritual weapons, and implementing these strategies, we can experience the true freedom and victory that Christ offers. The chains will be shattered, and the captives will be set free.

Warfare Prayer

1. In the mighty name of Jesus, I declare that I am no longer a captive to strongholds; I am set free!

2. By the power of the Holy Spirit, I break the chains of addiction and declare my deliverance.

3. Every negative thought pattern in my mind is dismantled, and I am transformed by the renewing of my mind in Christ Jesus.

4. I take authority over every stronghold of fear and anxiety in my life; you have no power here!

5. In Jesus' name, I declare that I am an overcomer, and no stronghold can hold me back.

6. I release the Word of God as a two-edged sword to cut down every stronghold that opposes His truth.

7. By the blood of Jesus, I am cleansed from all unrighteousness, and the enemy's accusations have no place in my life.

8. I cast down every imagination and every high thing that exalts itself against the knowledge of God in my thoughts.

9. I declare that the light of God's truth exposes and shatters every hidden stronghold in my heart.

10. By faith, I put on the full armor of God, and no weapon formed against me shall prosper.

11. In Jesus' name, I declare my authority over principalities and powers that seek to establish strongholds.

12. I bind the spirit of addiction and release the spirit of self-control, discipline, and freedom in Christ.

13. I declare that I am more than a conqueror through Him who loves me, and no stronghold can stand against His love.

14. I break every generational stronghold that has plagued my family line, and I release a legacy of freedom and faith.

15. I command every demonic influence that has built strongholds in my life to flee in the name of Jesus.

16. I release the power of forgiveness, and every stronghold of bitterness and unforgiveness is dismantled.

17. I declare that my mind is a sanctuary for the Holy Spirit, and no stronghold can defile it.

18. By the authority of Jesus' name, I command the walls of every stronghold to crumble and fall.

19. I declare my complete dependence on God's grace and His strength to overcome every stronghold.

20. I rebuke the spirit of doubt and declare my unwavering faith in God's promises.

21. In Jesus' name, I declare that I am an instrument of righteousness, and sin shall not have dominion over me.

22. I release the power of worship and praise to dismantle strongholds and usher in the presence of God.

23. I declare that I am a vessel of honor, sanctified and useful for the Master's work.

24. By the authority of the blood of Jesus, I am cleansed from all guilt and shame associated with past strongholds.

25. I command every spirit of addiction to loose its grip on my life and leave in the name of Jesus.

26. I declare that my heart is a dwelling place for the Holy Spirit, and He reigns supreme.

27. I renounce every pact, vow, or covenant made with the enemy, and I break their influence over my life.

28. In Jesus' name, I declare that I am a warrior of light, dispelling darkness and strongholds wherever I go.

29. I release the healing power of God to restore every area of my life affected by strongholds.

30. I declare that the joy of the Lord is my strength, and no stronghold can steal my joy.

31. By the authority of Jesus' name, I cast out every unclean spirit that has established a stronghold in my life.

32. I declare my identity as a child of God, and no stronghold can define me except His love.

33. I release the fire of the Holy Spirit to burn away every impurity and stronghold in my life.

34. I declare that I am seated with Christ in heavenly places, far above all principalities and strongholds.

35. By faith, I receive the power to trample on serpents and scorpions, and nothing shall by any means harm me.

36. I declare that I am anointed with the oil of gladness, and despair has no place in my heart.

37. I release the sound of victory, and every stronghold must yield to the triumphant shout of praise.

38. In Jesus' name, I declare that I am filled with the love of God, casting out all fear associated with strongholds.

39. I declare that I am a vessel of honor, sanctified and set apart for God's purposes, free from the grip of strongholds.

40. I seal these declarations with the blood of Jesus, and I trust in His power to keep me free from every stronghold. Amen!

Chapter 16

Unmasking Deception:
Discernment in the Dark

In the realm of spiritual warfare, discernment is the razor-sharp sword that cuts through the web of deception spun by the powers of darkness. In this chapter, we delve into the depths of discernment from a Christian perspective, focusing on the critical importance of honing this gift for navigating the spiritual battlefield. As midnight warriors, our ability to unmask deception is not merely a skill but a divine mandate.

The Nature of Deception

Deception is the crafty artistry of the enemy, Satan, who is often referred to as the "father of lies" in Christian theology. It's crucial to understand that deception doesn't always come in the form of blatant falsehoods; more often, it wears the cloak of half-truths, subtle distortions, and twisted interpretations of God's Word. As midnight warriors, we are called to be discerning, not just of the obvious traps but also the snares that masquerade as truth.

The Gift of Discernment

Discernment is not a mere human faculty; it is a divine gift imparted by the Holy Spirit. The Apostle Paul, in his letter to the Corinthians, speaks of the "discerning of spirits" as one of the spiritual gifts (1 Corinthians 12:10). This gift enables us to see beyond the natural realm into the spiritual, exposing hidden agendas, false teachings, and demonic influences.

Sharpening the Blade of Discernment

1. Deepening Your Relationship with God: Discernment is intimately connected to your walk with God. The closer you draw to Him through prayer, worship, and studying His Word, the sharper your discernment becomes. In the darkness of midnight, it is your communion with God that will illuminate the path of truth.

2. Testing the Spirits: The Apostle John admonishes believers to "test the spirits to see whether they are from God" (1 John 4:1). Midnight warriors must be diligent in testing every message, vision, or revelation they encounter. Discernment involves asking tough questions and seeking confirmation from the Holy Spirit.

3. The Word as Your Plumb Line: The Bible is the unerring plumb line by which all teachings and prophecies should be measured. Deception often begins by twisting Scripture, as the enemy did in the wilderness when tempting Jesus. Familiarize yourself with the Word to recognize distortions and misinterpretations.

161

4. Praying for Discernment: James 1:5 assures us that if we lack wisdom, we can ask God who gives generously. Praying for discernment is not a sign of weakness but an acknowledgment of our dependence on God's guidance. As midnight warriors, we should pray fervently for this gift.

5. Community and Accountability: God often imparts discernment through the counsel of fellow believers. Seek out trusted spiritual mentors and advisors who can offer insights and confirmation when needed. Accountability in discernment helps prevent personal biases from clouding your judgment.

Navigating the Fog of Spiritual Warfare

Midnight warfare is rife with spiritual fog, where the lines between light and darkness blur. It is precisely in these moments that discernment becomes a lifeline. Consider these scenarios:

1. Discerning False Prophets: The New Testament warns of false prophets who will arise with deceptive signs and wonders (Matthew 24:24). Discernment is your shield against being led astray by charismatic but false leaders.

2. Identifying Spiritual Attacks: Not all trials and tribulations are purely natural; some may be orchestrated by the enemy. Discernment allows you

to differentiate between the refining hand of God and the attacks of the adversary.

3. Unmasking Hidden Agendas: In the midst of spiritual warfare, the enemy often conceals his true intentions. Discernment helps you see beyond the surface and discern the motives behind actions and words.

4. Exposing Doctrinal Error: Deceptive teachings can infiltrate even the most well-intentioned congregations. With discernment, you can recognize doctrinal errors that could lead many astray.

The Risks of Ignoring Discernment

Failure to cultivate discernment can have dire consequences. Ignoring this vital gift can lead to spiritual deception, confusion, and ineffectiveness in spiritual warfare. Without discernment, you may unwittingly cooperate with the very forces you seek to combat.

The Lamp of Discernment

In the dark, treacherous terrain of midnight warfare, discernment is the lamp that guides our steps. It is the gift that unveils the hidden, separates the counterfeit from the genuine, and ensures that our prayers and actions align with God's will. As midnight warriors, we must fervently seek, nurture, and rely on the discernment given by the Holy Spirit. With discernment as our ally, we become formidable opponents to the powers of darkness, unmasking their deceptions and advancing God's kingdom in the midnight hour.

Warfare Prayer

1. In the mighty name of Jesus, I declare that the gift of discernment is activated within me, enabling me to unmask every form of deception.

2. I decree and declare that I am a midnight warrior, equipped with the divine gift of discernment to expose the works of darkness.

3. By the authority of Jesus Christ, I rebuke and bind all spirits of deception and falsehood that seek to infiltrate my life and the lives of others.

4. I declare that I am rooted in God's Word, and I will not be swayed by distorted interpretations or twisted teachings.

5. In the name of Jesus, I reject all half-truths and subtle lies that the enemy tries to present to me.

6. I decree that my discernment is sharpened daily as I draw closer to God through prayer, worship, and meditation on His Word.

7. By the power of the Holy Spirit, I discern the true nature of every spiritual influence and test every spirit to see if it is from God.

8. I declare that I have a discerning heart and a spirit of wisdom to navigate the complexities of spiritual warfare.

9. In Jesus' name, I pray for a supernatural revelation of God's truth, exposing all forms of deception in my life and the lives of those I intercede for.

10. I bind and break the power of every deceptive spirit that attempts to cloud my judgment and lead me astray.

11. I declare that I am a watchman on the wall, discerning the signs of the times and alert to the enemy's schemes.

12. By the authority of Jesus, I discern the motives and intentions of those around me, exposing any hidden agendas that are not in alignment with God's will.

13. I decree that I will not be deceived by false prophets or charismatic leaders who do not speak in line with God's Word.

14. In Jesus' name, I reject all forms of spiritual manipulation and control, discerning the tactics of the enemy.

15. I declare that the light of discernment shines brightly in my life, dispelling the darkness of deception.

16. By the power of the Holy Spirit, I expose and dismantle every stronghold of deceit that the enemy has erected.

17. I decree that I am discerning of the subtle whispers of the enemy and will not be led astray by his cunning schemes.

18. In Jesus' name, I discern the difference between God's refining work and the attacks of the adversary, standing firm in faith.

19. I declare that I am a defender of sound doctrine, discerning and rejecting any teachings that deviate from God's Word.

20. By the authority of Jesus Christ, I discern the spiritual atmosphere around me and release the presence of God to dispel darkness.

21. I bind and rebuke all spirits of confusion and deception that may try to cloud my mind or heart.

22. I decree that I have the discernment to recognize the voice of God and distinguish it from all other voices.

23. In Jesus' name, I discern the true intentions of those who come into my life, ensuring that their influence aligns with God's purpose.

24. I declare that I am a vessel of discernment, uncovering the hidden truths that the enemy seeks to conceal.

25. By the power of the Holy Spirit, I discern the divine strategies and plans of God, aligning myself with His purposes.

26. I bind and break all deception in the spiritual realm, rendering the enemy's tactics ineffective.

27. I decree that I am a guardian of righteousness and integrity, discerning and exposing all forms of dishonesty.

28. In Jesus' name, I discern the spiritual battles that rage around me and engage in warfare with clarity and authority.

29. I declare that I am an overcomer through the discernment granted to me by the Holy Spirit.

30. By the authority of Jesus Christ, I discern the hidden traps and snares of the enemy, avoiding them with divine insight.

31. I bind and rebuke all spirits of fear and doubt that may hinder my discernment.

32. I decree that I am filled with the discernment to navigate the spiritual battlefield with confidence and precision.

33. In Jesus' name, I discern the divine opportunities and assignments that God places before me, seizing them for His glory.

34. I declare that I am a vessel of divine revelation, uncovering the mysteries of God's kingdom and exposing the enemy's secrets.

35. By the power of the Holy Spirit, I discern the path of righteousness and walk in it, avoiding all detours into deception.

36. I bind and break all generational patterns of deception, releasing my family and descendants into the freedom of discernment.

37. I decree that I am a beacon of light in the darkness, illuminating the way for others to discern the truth.

38. In Jesus' name, I discern the divine connections and relationships that God orchestrates, guarding against harmful associations.

39. I declare that I am a warrior of discernment, standing strong against the schemes of the enemy.

40. By the authority of Jesus Christ, I release a wave of discernment over the body of Christ, empowering believers to unmask deception and walk in the light of God's truth.

Chapter 17

Holy Ghost Uprising:
Empowered by the Spirit

In the realm of spiritual warfare, there is no greater ally, no mightier force, than the Holy Spirit. The very presence of God, the Third Person of the Holy Trinity, the Spirit of Truth, is not merely a bystander in our battles against the forces of darkness. Instead, He is the divine empowerment that ignites the midnight warrior's heart and guides their every move. This chapter is an exploration of the profound relationship between the believer and the Holy Spirit, a partnership that forms the core of effective spiritual warfare.

The Holy Spirit: God's Divine Agent

To understand the Holy Ghost Uprising, we must first grasp the nature and role of the Holy Spirit in the believer's life. In the Christian faith, the Holy Spirit is seen as the Paraclete, the Comforter, and the Counselor sent by Christ Himself to empower, teach, and guide His followers. He is not an abstract concept but a living and active presence within the hearts of believers.

The Indwelling Presence

The Holy Spirit takes up residence within every believer, making their body His temple. This indwelling is not a distant or occasional experience; it is an ongoing, intimate relationship with the divine. It's a truth that can't be emphasized enough: as a midnight warrior, you are never alone in your battles. The Spirit of God is always with you, ready to empower and embolden you.

The Spirit's Role in Warfare

The Holy Spirit is not a passive observer in the spiritual battle; He is the dynamic force that empowers every aspect of the midnight warrior's life and ministry. When engaged in warfare, it's crucial to understand how the Spirit operates in this context.

Discernment and Guidance

One of the Spirit's primary roles is to provide discernment and guidance. In the thick of battle, He illuminates the strategies of the enemy and reveals hidden truths. The Spirit gives you the ability to see beyond the natural and perceive the spiritual realm, allowing you to make informed decisions and take strategic actions.

Supernatural Empowerment

In the face of seemingly insurmountable odds, the Holy Spirit imparts supernatural power. This isn't a power for personal glory but for God's glory and the advancement of His kingdom. It's the power that enabled David to defeat Goliath, Daniel to survive the lion's den, and the apostles to turn the world upside down with the Gospel.

Prayer and Intercession

The Holy Spirit is the ultimate prayer partner. In times of intense warfare, when words fail and the heart groans, He intercedes on our behalf with groanings too deep for words (Romans 8:26). This is the language of the Spirit—a supernatural form of communication that transcends our human limitations.

Activating the Holy Spirit's Power

To fully experience the Holy Ghost Uprising, one must actively engage with the Holy Spirit. It's not enough to acknowledge His presence; you must invite Him to take the lead in your spiritual battles. Here are some practical steps to activate His power:

Surrender and Yield

Submit your will and desires to the Holy Spirit. This surrender is not a sign of weakness but of trust and dependence on the One who knows the battle plan and has the power to execute it.

Prayer and Fasting

Engage in fervent prayer and fasting. These spiritual disciplines sharpen your sensitivity to the Spirit's leading and amplify His power within you.

Word of God

Immerse yourself in the Word of God. The Spirit uses Scripture to reveal truths, provide guidance, and strengthen your faith. The more you know God's Word, the more effectively you can wield the sword of the Spirit (Ephesians 6:17).

Worship and Praise

Engage in worship and praise. The Spirit is drawn to an atmosphere of adoration and reverence. As you lift up the name of Jesus, the presence of the Holy Spirit becomes tangible, filling you with supernatural strength.

Unity in the Body

Seek unity with fellow believers. The Spirit's power is often most evident when believers come together in one accord. Corporate prayer and worship create an environment where the Spirit's power can flow freely.

Real-Life Testimonies

To illustrate the impact of the Holy Ghost Uprising, let's delve into real-life testimonies of believers who have experienced the Holy Spirit's power in their warfare against the powers of darkness.

Testimony 1: Spiritual Discernment

Sarah, a midnight warrior, found herself in a situation where she needed to discern the source of a troubling dream. She prayed fervently, inviting the Holy Spirit to reveal the truth. In a moment of clarity, she realized the dream was an attempt by the enemy to instill fear. With this revelation, she boldly declared victory over the enemy's schemes, and peace flooded her heart.

Testimony 2: Supernatural Empowerment

Mark faced a daunting battle against addiction. Despite numerous attempts to break free, he remained bound. One night, in the depth of despair, he cried out to the Holy Spirit for help. An overwhelming surge of strength and resolve filled him, enabling him to break the chains of addiction and walk in newfound freedom.

Testimony 3: Intercession and Miracles

A group of believers gathered for a midnight prayer vigil to intercede for a family member stricken with a life-threatening illness. As they prayed in the Spirit, a supernatural peace enveloped them. Miraculously, the next morning, the doctors reported an unexplainable improvement in the patient's condition, and the family rejoiced in God's healing power.

The Call to Uprising

The Holy Ghost Uprising is not an option; it's a divine mandate for every midnight warrior. It's a call to rise above the limitations of human strength and tap into the boundless power of the Holy Spirit. It's an invitation to engage in spiritual warfare with unwavering confidence, knowing that victory is assured through the Spirit's empowerment.

As you embark on this journey of Holy Ghost Uprising, remember that the Spirit within you is greater than any adversary you may face. His power knows no bounds, and with Him as your guide and strength, you are destined for triumph in the midnight hour. So, equip yourself with the full armor of God, take up the sword of the Spirit, and let the Holy Ghost Uprising begin!

Warfare Prayer

1. In the name of Jesus, I declare that I am filled with the Holy Spirit, and His presence empowers me for spiritual warfare.

2. Holy Spirit, I yield to Your guidance and discernment in every battle I face. You reveal hidden strategies of the enemy.

3. I decree that the Holy Spirit's supernatural power flows through me, enabling me to overcome every obstacle and opposition.

4. In the name of Jesus, I declare that I am a vessel of divine authority, and I walk in the victory of Christ.

5. Holy Spirit, I invite You to intercede on my behalf with groanings too deep for words, aligning my prayers with God's will.

6. I boldly proclaim that the Word of God is my sword, and I wield it effectively against the forces of darkness.

7. I declare unity among fellow believers, and together, we form a powerful, unbreakable spiritual bond in the name of Jesus.

8. Holy Spirit, I acknowledge Your presence in my life, and I surrender my will to Your guidance and direction.

9. In Jesus' name, I declare that my prayers are effective and impactful, shaking the foundations of the enemy's plans.

10. I decree that I am more than a conqueror through Christ who strengthens me, and I fearlessly confront spiritual strongholds.

11. Holy Spirit, I immerse myself in the Word of God, and Your wisdom and revelation flow through me.

12. I declare that my worship and praise create an atmosphere where the presence of the Holy Spirit is tangible.

13. In the name of Jesus, I rebuke all fear, doubt, and insecurity, and I embrace the boldness that comes from the Spirit.

14. I proclaim that I am a part of the Holy Ghost Uprising, and I rise above human limitations in spiritual warfare.

15. Holy Spirit, I thank You for Your indwelling presence, which gives me confidence and assurance in every battle.

16. I declare that I am a midnight warrior, fully equipped with the armor of God, ready to engage the enemy.

17. In Jesus' name, I break every chain and shackle that the enemy has placed on my life or my loved ones.

18. I decree that I walk in divine health and wholeness, and I reject all attacks on my physical and spiritual well-being.

19. Holy Spirit, I invite You to reveal the hidden mysteries of the spiritual realm, granting me insight and revelation.

20. I boldly declare that I am an overcomer, and no weapon formed against me shall prosper.

21. In the name of Jesus, I release supernatural healing and restoration into my life and the lives of those I pray for.

22. I proclaim that I am a vigilant watchman, discerning the times and seasons in the Spirit.

23. I decree that my prayers usher in the presence of angels, who fight alongside me in the heavenly realms.

24. Holy Spirit, I ask for divine downloads of wisdom and understanding to navigate the challenges of spiritual warfare.

25. In Jesus' name, I declare that I am a part of a Holy Ghost Uprising that is shaking the kingdom of darkness.

26. I rebuke all deception and falsehood, and I embrace the truth that sets me free.

27. I boldly proclaim victory in every area of my life, knowing that the Spirit within me is greater than any adversary.

28. In the name of Jesus, I release the power of praise and worship, filling the atmosphere with divine presence.

29. I decree that I am a living testimony of the Holy Ghost Uprising, displaying God's glory through my life.

30. I thank the Holy Spirit for His guidance, empowerment, and constant presence in my spiritual battles.

31. In Jesus' name, I declare that I am a fearless warrior, unshaken by the schemes of the enemy.

32. I proclaim that I have the mind of Christ, and I am led by the Spirit into all truth and wisdom.

33. I rebuke every hindrance and obstacle in my path, and I walk in the divine favor and grace of God.

34. Holy Spirit, I invite You to release signs and wonders in my life and ministry, demonstrating God's power.

35. I decree that my prayers are like incense before God's throne, pleasing and acceptable in His sight.

36. In the name of Jesus, I release the fire of the Holy Spirit to consume all darkness and evil in my life and surroundings.

37. I declare that I am a vessel of love and compassion, extending God's grace to those in need.

38. I proclaim that I am an instrument of peace, bringing reconciliation and unity in the body of Christ.

39. Holy Spirit, I ask for divine appointments and opportunities to share the Gospel and lead others to Christ.

40. In Jesus' name, I seal these declarations with faith and authority, knowing that the Holy Ghost Uprising is unstoppable, and I am a victorious warrior in the kingdom of God. Amen!

Chapter 18

The Midnight Courts:
Presenting Your Case

In the realm of spiritual warfare, the concept of "The Midnight Courts" is a profound and powerful one. It represents a divine courtroom where believers can present their cases, make petitions, and seek justice in the supernatural realm. This chapter delves deep into the mystical and often misunderstood aspects of engaging with The Midnight Courts from a Christian perspective.

The Midnight Hour and Its Significance

Before we dive into the intricacies of The Midnight Courts, it's essential to understand the significance of the midnight hour in the spiritual realm. Midnight is a time when the natural world is at its darkest and quietest. In this physical darkness, the spiritual world becomes more active. It is a time when the powers of darkness are most active, but it's also a time when your spiritual authority can shine the brightest.

The Divine Courtroom

Imagine a grand, celestial courtroom where the Almighty God presides as the righteous Judge. This is The Midnight Courts. It's a place where justice, righteousness, and divine order prevail. The Bible often portrays God as a Judge, and this concept is not limited to the earthly courts. In Psalm 89:14, we read, "Righteousness and justice are the foundation of your throne; steadfast love and faithfulness go before you."

The Role of the Accuser

In the spiritual realm, there is an accuser, Satan, who "accuses the brethren before our God day and night" (Revelation 12:10). He seeks to bring charges against believers, pointing out their faults and weaknesses. The Midnight Courts serve as the platform where these accusations are heard. However, the good news is that we have an Advocate in Jesus Christ who defends us. As it says in 1 John 2:1, "We have an Advocate with the Father, Jesus Christ the righteous."

Presenting Your Case

When we engage with The Midnight Courts, we step into the role of both the petitioner and the defendant. As believers, we have the privilege of presenting our cases before God. These cases can encompass a wide range of issues, from personal struggles to interceding for others or even praying for nations. Here's how you can effectively present your case:

1. Confession and Repentance: Begin by acknowledging any sins or shortcomings in your life. Confession and repentance are essential as they remove any legal grounds that the accuser might have.

2. Claiming the Blood of Jesus: Plead the blood of Jesus over your life and your case. The blood of Jesus is your ultimate defense, and it speaks of forgiveness, redemption, and protection.

3. Declaration of God's Promises: Bring forth God's promises that are relevant to your case. Scriptures are your legal evidence in The Midnight Courts. For example, if you are facing sickness, declare Isaiah 53:5, "By His stripes, I am healed."

4. Intercession and Petition: The Midnight Courts are not just about personal matters. You can intercede for others, bringing their cases before God. Pray for the salvation of loved ones, healing for the sick, or peace in conflict zones.

5. Worship and Thanksgiving: Engage in worship and thanksgiving. This shifts the atmosphere in the courtroom. Remember that God inhabits the praises of His people (Psalm 22:3).

The Angelic Witnesses

In The Midnight Courts, there are angelic witnesses. These celestial beings testify on your behalf as you present your case. Hebrews 1:14 tells us that angels are "ministering spirits sent forth to minister for those who will inherit salvation." They actively work to bring about God's purposes in response to your prayers.

The Verdict and Enforcement

As you present your case, trust in God's perfect timing. He is the righteous Judge who will render a verdict. Sometimes, the answers to your prayers may not be immediate, but rest assured that God is working behind the scenes.

Once the verdict is issued, it's essential to continue praying and enforcing that verdict in the earthly realm. This may involve taking action in faith, making declarations, and standing firm on God's promises.

The Midnight Courts are a profound aspect of spiritual warfare that allows believers to engage in the heavenly legal system. By presenting your case with faith, repentance, and the authority of Christ, you can experience breakthroughs, deliverance, and the manifestation of God's justice in your life and the lives of others. Remember, in the spiritual realm, the midnight hour is a time of divine appointments and supernatural encounters. Embrace it with confidence and expect God to move mightily on your behalf.

Warfare Prayer

1. In the mighty name of Jesus, I boldly approach The Midnight Courts, where righteousness and justice reign supreme.

2. I declare that I am covered by the precious blood of Jesus, and no accusation against me shall prosper.

3. By the authority given to me in Christ, I repent of all my sins and shortcomings, and I stand blameless before the Judge of all.

4. In Jesus' name, I present my case for healing, and I claim Isaiah 53:5, "By His stripes, I am healed."

5. I bring my loved ones before The Midnight Courts, praying for their salvation, deliverance, and restoration.

6. I declare that I am a child of God, and no weapon formed against me shall prevail.

7. By faith, I call upon the angelic witnesses to testify on my behalf, for they are sent by God to minister for my good.

8. I reject all accusations of the enemy, for I am redeemed and justified by the blood of the Lamb.

9. I declare Psalm 91:11 over my life, "For He shall give His angels charge over me, to keep me in all my ways."

10. I stand in the authority of Jesus and decree divine protection over my family, home, and possessions.

11. I present my case for financial breakthrough, and I claim Philippians 4:19, "And my God shall supply all my needs according to His riches in glory by Christ Jesus."

12. I release the power of worship and thanksgiving in The Midnight Courts, knowing that God inhabits my praises.

13. I pray for nations in turmoil, and I declare peace, unity, and righteousness to prevail.

14. I plead the blood of Jesus over my mind, casting down every thought that exalts itself against the knowledge of God.

15. I bind every spirit of fear, anxiety, and depression, for I have the peace of God that surpasses all understanding.

16. In Jesus' name, I break the chains of addiction and declare freedom for all captives.

17. I decree that my prayers are powerful and effective, and they bring about supernatural breakthroughs.

18. I stand as an intercessor for the persecuted church, pleading for their safety and strength.

19. I release healing into the lives of those who are sick and suffering, for Jesus is the Great Physician.

20. I take authority over every demonic stronghold in my life, tearing them down in the name of Jesus.

21. I declare that I am more than a conqueror through Christ who loves me.

22. I speak restoration into broken relationships and families, declaring God's healing and reconciliation.

23. I rebuke every storm in my life, and I command peace and stillness in every area.

24. I declare supernatural wisdom and revelation to guide my steps in every decision.

25. I release the fire of the Holy Spirit to consume every work of darkness in my life.

26. I pray for the leaders of my nation, asking God for wisdom, integrity, and righteous governance.

27. I speak blessings and favor over my workplace and career, knowing that I am a light in the darkness.

28. I decree divine alignment in my spiritual walk, that I may fulfill my God-given purpose.

29. I declare victory over generational curses, for I am a new creation in Christ Jesus.

30. I bind the spirit of procrastination and declare a season of productivity and creativity.

31. I release the love of God to overflow from my heart, touching the lives of those around me.

32. I rebuke the devourer in my finances, and I claim abundance and prosperity in Jesus' name.

33. I pray for the peace of Jerusalem and declare God's protection over the Holy Land.

34. I take authority over every nightmare and demonic dream, commanding them to flee.

35. I declare that my prayers are like incense before the throne of God, pleasing and acceptable.

36. I release the spirit of unity and harmony in my church, that we may be a shining light in our community.

37. I bind the spirit of division and declare reconciliation in relationships that have been strained.

38. I declare that my faith is unwavering, and I trust in God's perfect timing.

39. I pray for a revival in my city, declaring that the light of Christ will shine brightly.

40. I seal these declarations in the name of Jesus, knowing that His authority and power are at work in my life and in The Midnight Courts. Amen.

Chapter 19

Praise as a Weapon: Crushing the Enemy's Plans

In the heart of midnight, where the darkness looms and the powers of evil seem to gather their strength, one of the most potent weapons in the arsenal of a midnight warrior is praise. Praise is not just an expression of joy or gratitude; it is a spiritual weapon that has the power to shatter the schemes and plans of the enemy. In this chapter, we will delve deep into the transformative and devastating force of praise in the realm of spiritual warfare.

The Dynamics of Praise

Praise is a concept deeply rooted in Christianity. It's the act of acknowledging and extolling the greatness, goodness, and majesty of God. It's an act of surrender and adoration that transcends our circumstances. But what makes praise such a formidable weapon in spiritual warfare?

1. Shift in Focus: When we engage in praise, our focus shifts from our problems to the greatness of God. We are essentially saying, "You are bigger than this situation, Lord." This shift in focus disrupts the enemy's strategy to keep us fixated on our troubles, thus dismantling their plans.

2. Atmospheric Change: Praise has the power to change the spiritual atmosphere. Just as negative thoughts and words can create an environment conducive to the enemy's work, praise ushers in the presence of God, creating an atmosphere that is hostile to demonic forces.

3. Demonstrating Faith: Praise is an expression of faith. When we praise God in the midst of adversity, we are declaring our trust in His sovereignty and goodness. This act of faith unnerves the enemy, as it demonstrates our unwavering belief in God's power to intervene.

The Sound of Victory

In many battles, including those in the Bible, the sound of victory was often accompanied by music and praise. Perhaps the most famous example is found in the story of Jehoshaphat in 2 Chronicles 20. When the armies of Judah faced an overwhelming alliance of enemies, Jehoshaphat did not send out his soldiers first. Instead, he appointed singers to lead the army, singing praises to God. As they praised, confusion struck their enemies, leading to their defeat.

This account teaches us a profound lesson: praise is not just a reaction to victory; it's the sound of victory itself. When we praise God in the midst of our battles, we are declaring that the battle belongs to Him, and the victory is assured.

Weapons of Praise

Let's explore some specific ways in which praise can be employed as a weapon to thwart the enemy's plans:

1. Singing in the Night: Midnight is the perfect time for a symphony of praise. Singing praises to God in the stillness of the night can break the grip of fear and oppression. The enemy hates the sound of worship echoing through the darkness.

2. Prophetic Declarations: Combine your praise with prophetic declarations. Proclaim God's promises over your life and circumstances. Declare His Word boldly, for it is a double-edged sword that pierces through the enemy's schemes.

3. Dancing Before the Lord: King David, a man after God's own heart, was known for his exuberant dancing in worship. Dancing before the Lord can release a powerful wave of praise that scatters the enemy's plans.

4. Instruments of Warfare: Consider using musical instruments in your midnight praise. The sound of instruments can amplify the intensity of your worship and disorient the forces of darkness.

Praise That Confounds the Enemy

In the book of Acts, we find another striking example of praise as a weapon. Paul and Silas, imprisoned in the darkest hours of the night, chose to pray and sing hymns to God. Their praise was so powerful that it caused an earthquake, shaking the foundations of the prison and breaking their chains. This supernatural event not only secured their freedom but also led to the salvation of their jailer and his household.

This story teaches us that praise has the capacity to break chains, not only in our lives but also in the lives of those around us. It can open doors and create opportunities for the Gospel to shine forth, even in the darkest of circumstances.

The Challenge of Midnight Praise

It's important to acknowledge that praising God in the midnight hour, especially when facing intense spiritual warfare, can be a challenge. The enemy will try to fill your mind with doubts, fears, and distractions. However, it's precisely in these moments that your praise becomes a fierce weapon.

Remember that your praise doesn't have to be perfect; it just needs to be genuine. God sees your heart and hears your cries, even when your words may falter. The sincerity of your praise is what makes it effective.

A Lifestyle of Praise

To truly harness the power of praise as a weapon in spiritual warfare, it must become a lifestyle. Incorporate praise into your daily routine, not just as a reaction to difficulties, but as a continuous expression of your love and reverence for God.

As you make praise a habit, you'll find that the enemy's plans are continually disrupted, and the presence of God surrounds you like a shield. Your life will become a testimony to the world of the victorious power of praise in the darkest hours.

In the realm of spiritual warfare, praise is not a passive response; it is an aggressive weapon that crushes the enemy's plans. It shifts the focus from our problems to the greatness of God, changes the spiritual atmosphere, and demonstrates unwavering faith. Praise is the sound of victory, the key to breaking chains, and the catalyst for supernatural breakthroughs.

So, as a midnight warrior, take up this weapon of praise. Let your voice rise in the darkest of nights, and watch as the enemy's plans crumble before the majesty of our Almighty God. In praise, you will find the strength to overcome, the joy of victory, and the assurance that no plan of darkness can stand against the radiant light of Christ.

Warfare Prayer

1. In the mighty name of Jesus, I declare that praise is my weapon, and I will wield it with boldness and faith.

2. By the authority of Jesus Christ, I shift my focus from my problems to the greatness of God through praise.

3. I decree that as I praise God, the spiritual atmosphere around me is transformed, and the enemy's plans are disrupted.

4. In Jesus' name, I declare that my praise demonstrates unwavering faith in God's sovereignty and goodness.

5. I proclaim that my praise is the sound of victory over every scheme of darkness.

6. By the power of the Holy Spirit, I release songs of praise in the midnight hour, scattering the forces of evil.

7. I speak prophetic declarations over my life, declaring God's promises and watching them manifest.

8. I will dance before the Lord, and my dance will release a wave of praise that confounds the enemy.

9. In Jesus' name, I declare that my praise is a spiritual weapon that breaks chains and sets captives free.

10. I take up musical instruments as instruments of warfare, and the sound of praise will pierce through the darkness.

11. By the blood of Jesus, I command every stronghold of the enemy to crumble as I praise the Almighty.

12. I declare that my praise is a sweet fragrance to God, and He delights in my worship.

13. In Jesus' name, I take authority over every spirit of fear and distraction that tries to hinder my praise.

14. I decree that my praise creates an environment where God's presence reigns supreme, and demons tremble.

15. By the Word of God, I declare that I am a worshipper in spirit and truth, and my praise is genuine and powerful.

16. I take authority over every spirit of doubt and unbelief that seeks to silence my praise.

17. In Jesus' name, I declare that my praise is a key that opens doors and paves the way for God's blessings.

18. I proclaim that my praise is a source of supernatural breakthroughs in every area of my life.

19. By the power of the Holy Spirit, I release the earthquake of praise, shaking the foundations of every prison in my life.

20. I declare that my praise breaks every chain of bondage and sets me free to walk in the fullness of God's purpose.

21. In the name of Jesus, I release praise that brings salvation to those around me, drawing them into the Kingdom of God.

22. I take authority over every thought and distraction that tries to hinder my praise, and I cast them down.

23. By the authority of Jesus' name, I declare that my praise is a beacon of hope in the darkest of times.

24. I decree that my praise is a testimony to the world of the victorious power of Christ.

25. In Jesus' name, I declare that my praise is a lifestyle, a continual expression of my love and reverence for God.

26. I proclaim that the enemy's plans are continually disrupted as I make praise a habit in my life.

27. By the blood of Jesus, I silence every voice of discouragement that tries to stifle my praise.

28. I take authority over every attack on my worship life and declare that I will praise God in all circumstances.

29. In Jesus' name, I release a torrent of praise that drowns out the enemy's accusations and lies.

30. I decree that my praise opens doors of favor and divine opportunities that no enemy can shut.

31. By the power of the Holy Spirit, I declare that my praise releases supernatural healing and restoration.

32. I proclaim that my praise is a declaration of victory over sickness, pain, and every form of oppression.

33. In Jesus' name, I declare that my praise is a powerful force that pushes back the darkness and ushers in God's light.

34. I take authority over every spirit of despair and declare that my praise brings hope and joy.

35. By the authority of Jesus' name, I release a symphony of praise that resonates with the heartbeat of heaven.

36. I decree that my praise brings divine revelation and understanding of God's purposes.

37. In Jesus' name, I declare that my praise is a sweet offering that ascends to the throne of grace.

38. I proclaim that my praise is a weapon that crushes the enemy's plans and scatters his forces.

39. By the power of the Holy Spirit, I declare that my praise is a source of strength and courage in times of spiritual warfare.

40. I take authority over every hindrance to my praise and declare that I will praise the Lord with all my heart, soul, and strength, for He is worthy of all honor and glory.

Chapter 20

Midnight Miracles:
Releasing Signs and Wonders

In the realm of spiritual warfare and the midnight hour, there exists a profound connection between the supernatural and the miraculous. It is at this sacred intersection that the faithful Midnight Warrior taps into the reservoir of divine power, unleashing signs and wonders that defy explanation and transcend the natural order. In this chapter, we delve deep into the art of invoking Midnight Miracles, exploring the biblical foundations, principles, and practices that can transform your midnight prayers into conduits of God's extraordinary intervention.

The Midnight Hour: A Divine Gateway

The midnight hour, often shrouded in darkness, holds a unique significance in the spiritual realm. It is a time when the physical world sleeps, but the supernatural realm awakens. The Bible is replete with instances where midnight played a pivotal role in ushering in God's miraculous interventions.

The Midnight Praise of Paul and Silas

Acts 16:25-26 recounts the story of Paul and Silas imprisoned in Philippi. At midnight, while confined in the inner prison, they prayed and sang hymns to God. Suddenly, a violent earthquake shook the prison, opening doors and loosening chains. This Midnight Miracle not only secured their release but also led to the salvation of the jailer and his household.

The Midnight Conversations of God

In the Old Testament, God often spoke to His servants in the stillness of the midnight hour. For instance, in 1 Samuel 3, God called Samuel by name three times during the night, revealing His divine plans. The midnight hour is, therefore, a time of divine encounters, when God unveils His purposes and releases His power.

Decrees and Declarations of Midnight Miracles

Midnight Miracles are not random happenings but rather deliberate acts of God in response to faith-filled prayers and declarations. Here are key elements to consider:

1. Aligning with God's Will

Effective midnight prayers for miracles begin with aligning your heart and desires with God's will. It is not about seeking miracles for personal gain but about advancing God's kingdom and demonstrating His glory.

2. Fervent and Faith-Filled Prayers

James 5:16b (NIV) reminds us, "The prayer of a righteous person is powerful and effective." In the midnight hour, prayers should be fervent and filled with unwavering faith. This is not the time for half-hearted petitions but for bold, audacious requests.

3. Prophetic Declarations

Prophetic declarations carry the power to shift spiritual atmospheres. Declare God's promises over your life, your family, your community, and your nation. Stand on His Word and proclaim His goodness.

4. Worship and Thanksgiving

Midnight Miracles often follow sincere acts of worship and thanksgiving. Like Paul and Silas, offer praises to God even in the midst of challenges. Gratitude opens the door for miracles.

Activating Midnight Miracles

Now, let's explore practical steps to activate Midnight Miracles in your life:

1. Set Apart a Midnight Watch

Allocate specific times during the midnight hour for prayer and meditation. Consistency in your midnight watch creates an atmosphere ripe for miracles.

2. Anointing and Consecration

Anoint yourself with holy oil as a symbol of consecration. Dedicate your midnight watch to God, inviting His presence to overshadow you.

3. Scripture Meditation

Meditate on passages that speak of God's miraculous power. Allow His Word to saturate your heart and build your faith.

4. Midnight Warfare Prayers

Engage in prayers that target specific needs and situations. Wage spiritual warfare against the forces of darkness that may be hindering your breakthrough.

Stories of Midnight Miracles

To inspire your faith, here are real-life testimonies of Midnight Miracles:

1. Healing at Midnight

Sarah, diagnosed with a terminal illness, began her midnight watch for healing. One fateful night, as she prayed with unwavering faith, she felt a warmth envelop her body. Medical tests later confirmed her miraculous healing, leaving doctors astounded.

2. Financial Breakthrough

John faced bankruptcy and the loss of his home. During his midnight prayer vigil, he declared God's promises of provision. Miraculously, a job opportunity and a financial windfall came his way, rescuing him from financial ruin.

Midnight Miracles are not limited by time or circumstance; they are limited only by your faith and willingness to engage in spiritual warfare at the midnight hour. Remember, it is not the darkness that defines the midnight watch, but the radiant presence of God that transforms it into a realm of supernatural encounters. As a Midnight Warrior, you possess the authority to release signs and wonders that will leave a lasting impact on your life and the lives of those around you. Embrace the midnight hour, for in it, God's miracles await your decree.

Warfare Prayer

1. In the name of Jesus, I declare that the midnight hour is a divine gateway for miracles and supernatural encounters.

2. I decree that I align my heart and desires with God's will, positioning myself for His extraordinary interventions.

3. By faith, I declare that my prayers in the midnight hour are powerful and effective, just as the Word of God promises.

4. In the authority of Jesus' name, I release prophetic declarations over my life and circumstances, shifting the spiritual atmosphere.

5. I declare that my midnight prayers are fervent, filled with unwavering faith, and bring forth miraculous manifestations.

6. By the blood of Jesus, I bind every force of darkness that seeks to hinder the release of Midnight Miracles.

7. I proclaim that my midnight watch is set apart for divine encounters, and God's presence overshadows me.

8. In the name of Jesus, I consecrate myself and my midnight watch, dedicating it to the glory of God.

9. I declare that I meditate on God's Word, allowing His promises of miracles to saturate my heart and build my faith.

10. By the authority vested in me through Jesus Christ, I wage spiritual warfare against every obstacle blocking my Midnight Miracles.

11. I declare that I am a Midnight Warrior, armed with the full armor of God, ready to stand firm and overcome.

12. In Jesus' name, I bind and cast out every spirit of doubt and unbelief that may try to hinder my faith.

13. I decree that my midnight prayers are a sweet fragrance before the throne of God, and He delights in answering them.

14. By faith, I release supernatural dreams and visions in the midnight hour, receiving divine revelations.

15. I declare that my midnight praise and worship unleash the power of God, breaking chains and releasing miracles.

16. I speak healing and restoration into my life and the lives of those I pray for in the midnight hour.

17. In the authority of Jesus' name, I release financial breakthroughs, declaring that all my needs are met according to God's riches in glory.

18. I proclaim that I am a vessel of God's glory, and His signs and wonders flow through me in the midnight hour.

19. I declare that the darkness of the midnight hour cannot overcome the light of Christ that shines within me.

20. By the blood of Jesus, I rebuke every spirit of fear and anxiety that may try to assail me during my midnight watch.

21. I speak peace and divine order into every area of my life, knowing that God is not the author of confusion.

22. In the name of Jesus, I release supernatural favor and open doors of opportunity in my midnight prayers.

23. I declare that angels are assigned to minister to me and to carry out God's divine assignments in the midnight hour.

24. I bind and dismantle every stronghold of the enemy that may be operating against me, declaring victory in Jesus' name.

25. By faith, I release signs and wonders in my family, community, and nation, impacting lives for Christ.

26. I declare that my midnight declarations shape the destiny of nations and influence the course of history.

27. I speak words of life and blessings over my loved ones, covering them in the protection of Jesus' name.

28. In the authority of Jesus, I command every storm in my life to be still, and I declare peace and tranquility.

29. I release supernatural provision, declaring that God's abundance flows into my life and circumstances.

30. I declare that I am a Midnight Watchman, standing guard over my sphere of influence and releasing God's blessings.

31. In Jesus' name, I release divine wisdom and revelation knowledge, unlocking mysteries in the midnight hour.

32. I proclaim that I am an overcomer by the blood of the Lamb and the word of my testimony.

33. I speak creative miracles into existence, believing that God can do the impossible in my midnight prayers.

34. By the authority of Jesus, I rebuke every sickness and infirmity, declaring divine health and healing.

35. I release the miraculous in my workplace, declaring that God's favor and excellence rest upon me.

36. In the name of Jesus, I declare that I am a carrier of God's glory, and signs and wonders follow me.

37. I speak restoration and reconciliation into broken relationships, believing for miraculous reconciliations.

38. By faith, I release supernatural breakthroughs in my ministry and calling, impacting lives for the kingdom.

39. I declare that I am an agent of revival, and the fire of God burns brightly within me in the midnight hour.

40. In Jesus' name, I seal these declarations, knowing that God's Word will not return void, but it will accomplish what it was sent to do. Amen!

Chapter 21

Supernatural Dreams and Visions:
Divine Revelations

In the realm of midnight warfare, there exists a profound and mysterious channel of communication between the divine and the human—a conduit through which God imparts His wisdom, guidance, and warnings. This channel is none other than the realm of supernatural dreams and visions. As midnight warriors, we are called to embrace and harness this extraordinary gift to gain insights into the spiritual battle that rages around us. In this chapter, we will delve deeply into the significance of supernatural dreams and visions from a Christian perspective, exploring their divine nature, their role in spiritual warfare, and practical steps to unlock their potential.

The Language of Dreams and Visions

Dreams and visions have been a means of divine communication throughout the Bible. From the patriarch Joseph, who interpreted Pharaoh's dream, to the apostle Peter, who received a vision of unclean animals, the Scriptures are replete with instances of God speaking through dreams and visions. These supernatural encounters serve as a unique language through which God imparts His messages, guidance, and revelations to His people.

Understanding the Divine Nature

Supernatural dreams and visions are not mere products of the subconscious mind or random neural firings during sleep; they are divine encounters with a purpose. In the stillness of the night, as we enter the realm of sleep, our minds become more receptive to the spiritual realm. It is in this vulnerable state that God often chooses to speak to us, unveiling mysteries and providing clarity on matters of importance.

These encounters can take various forms:

1. Prophetic Dreams: In these dreams, God may reveal future events, warn of impending danger, or give specific instructions. It was through a prophetic dream that Joseph was informed of the impending famine and how to prepare for it.

2. Visions: Unlike dreams, visions occur when we are awake but in a heightened state of spiritual sensitivity. Visions are like windows into the spiritual realm, allowing us to witness divine truths and realities beyond the physical.

3. Symbolic Dreams: God often communicates through symbols and metaphors in dreams. Understanding these symbols requires discernment and the guidance of the Holy Spirit.

The Role of Dreams and Visions in Spiritual Warfare

As midnight warriors, we must recognize the crucial role dreams and visions play in our battle against the powers of darkness. Here's how they contribute to our spiritual warfare arsenal:

1. Revelation of Hidden Schemes: God uses dreams and visions to unveil the hidden schemes and strategies of the enemy. Through these encounters, we gain insight into the enemy's plans, enabling us to counteract them effectively.

2. Confirmation of Divine Direction: When faced with critical decisions in our spiritual journey, dreams and visions can serve as confirmations of God's direction. They provide reassurance and guidance, helping us navigate the spiritual battlefield with confidence.

3. Intercession and Warfare: Supernatural dreams and visions often prompt us to intercede on behalf of individuals, cities, or nations. These encounters reveal the spiritual needs of specific regions and equip us to engage in targeted warfare through prayer.

4. Equipping for Battle: God may use dreams and visions to equip us with spiritual weapons, such as the sword of the Spirit or the armor of God. These encounters empower us for the battles we face in the midnight hour.

Practical Steps to Unlock the Potential

While supernatural dreams and visions are a divine gift, they can be cultivated and activated through faith and spiritual discipline. Here are practical steps to unlock their potential:

1. Dedicated Prayer: Begin by praying for the gift of discernment and the ability to receive divine dreams and visions. Dedicate time in your prayer life to seek these encounters.

2. Journaling: Keep a dream journal by your bedside. Record your dreams and visions immediately upon waking. Over time, patterns and themes may emerge, providing insight into God's messages.

3. Seek Interpretation: Seek the guidance of mature, spiritually discerning individuals or mentors who can help interpret the symbolism and meaning of your dreams and visions.

4. Fasting and Purification: Periods of fasting and consecration can increase your spiritual sensitivity, making you more receptive to divine communication.

5. Position Yourself: Position yourself in an atmosphere of worship and prayer before sleep. Invite the Holy Spirit to minister to you through dreams and visions.

6. Test the Spirits: Not all dreams and visions are from God. Test them against the Word of God and seek confirmation through prayer and counsel.

Supernatural dreams and visions are a powerful means through which God communicates with His people. In the context of midnight warfare, they serve as a strategic advantage, providing insights, guidance, and revelations that can ultimately lead to victory over the powers of darkness. Embrace this gift, nurture it with faith and prayer, and watch as the divine unfolds in the depths of the night, empowering you as a mighty midnight warrior.

Warfare Prayer

1. In the name of Jesus, I declare that my mind is open and receptive to supernatural dreams and visions from God.

2. I decree that I am a midnight warrior, equipped to receive divine revelations in my dreams.

3. By the authority of Jesus' name, I rebuke all hindrances and obstacles that may block my access to God's visions.

4. I declare that my dreams and visions are divinely inspired and filled with God's wisdom.

5. In Jesus' name, I rebuke all negative and deceptive dreams sent by the enemy; they have no power over me.

6. I declare that the Holy Spirit is my dream interpreter, and He guides me in understanding God's messages.

7. By the blood of Jesus, I cleanse my dream life from all impurities and defilements.

8. I decree that my dreams and visions align with the Word of God and His divine purpose for my life.

9. In the name of Jesus, I release the angels of revelation to minister to me in my dreams.

10. I declare that I am a watchman in the night, discerning the spiritual realm through dreams and visions.

11. By the authority of Jesus, I break every curse or hex that may affect my dreams and visions.

12. I declare that God's secrets and mysteries are revealed to me through supernatural dreams.

13. I decree that my dreams are a source of divine guidance and direction for my life.

14. In Jesus' name, I cancel all dreams of fear, anxiety, and confusion; they have no place in my life.

15. I declare that I am a carrier of divine messages through my dreams, impacting others for God's glory.

16. By the power of the Holy Spirit, I receive visions that empower me to overcome the powers of darkness.

17. I decree that God's prophetic dreams flow through me, foretelling His plans and purposes.

18. In the name of Jesus, I break every spiritual barrier that hinders clear communication with God in my dreams.

19. I declare that God's dreams for my life are greater than any earthly imagination.

20. I rebuke all nightmares and demonic attacks in my dreams; they are rendered powerless by the blood of Jesus.

21. By the authority of Christ, I pray for the discernment to distinguish between divine dreams and mere fantasies.

22. I decree that I am a dreamer of solutions, bringing answers to challenges in my life and the lives of others.

23. In Jesus' name, I declare that I am a vessel of God's creativity and innovation in my dreams.

24. I release the fire of the Holy Spirit upon my dream life, purifying it for God's use.

25. By the blood of Jesus, I dismantle and destroy all satanic strongholds in my dreams.

26. I decree that my dreams and visions release healing and restoration in my body, mind, and spirit.

27. In the name of Jesus, I bind and cast out all demonic spirits that attempt to infiltrate my dreams.

28. I declare that I am an overcomer in my dreams, defeating every spiritual adversary.

29. By the authority of Christ, I release blessings and favor through my dreams and visions.

30. I decree that my dreams are a source of supernatural provision and abundance.

31. In Jesus' name, I break the chains of doubt and unbelief that may hinder the manifestation of my dreams.

32. I declare that I am a dreamer of revival, awakening the hearts of many to God's truth.

33. By the power of the Holy Spirit, I pray for divine encounters with heavenly beings in my dreams.

34. I decree that my dreams release a fresh anointing and empowerment for my ministry and calling.

35. In the name of Jesus, I rebuke all dream thieves and dream assassins; they have no authority over me.

36. I declare that I am a dreamer of unity, bringing reconciliation and harmony in relationships.

37. By the authority of Christ, I release dreams of evangelism and salvation to the lost.

38. I decree that my dreams and visions are a source of divine protection and deliverance.

39. In Jesus' name, I pray for the restoration of lost dreams and the fulfillment of God's promises.

40. I declare that my life is a testimony of the power of supernatural dreams and visions, to the glory of God.

Chapter 22

The Bloodline Covenant: Securing Your Legacy

In the realms of spiritual warfare and midnight battles, there exists a sacred and potent concept that has been passed down through generations of faithful believers—a concept that carries with it the weight of divine promise and the power to secure your legacy for eternity. This concept is none other than the Bloodline Covenant, a profoundly meaningful and spiritually charged aspect of Christian faith and warfare.

The Genesis of the Bloodline Covenant

To delve into the depths of the Bloodline Covenant, we must first journey back to the beginning, to the very dawn of creation when God, in His infinite wisdom, crafted the blueprint of His divine plan. It was in the Garden of Eden where the initial threads of this covenant were woven into the fabric of human existence.

In Genesis, we encounter the first act of rebellion as Adam and Eve partook of the forbidden fruit, plunging humanity into sin and spiritual separation from God. Yet, even in the midst of their disobedience, God revealed a glimpse of His redemptive plan. He made garments of skin to clothe them, signifying the shedding of innocent blood to cover their shame.

This symbolic act foreshadowed the ultimate sacrifice—the shedding of the perfect, sinless blood of Jesus Christ to atone for the sins of humanity. It was the inauguration of the Bloodline Covenant, a covenant that would forever bind God to His people through the blood of His Son.

The Power of the Blood

The Bloodline Covenant is anchored in the belief that the blood of Jesus holds unparalleled power. It is not merely a symbolic gesture but a living, dynamic force that continues to flow through the veins of every believer. Let us explore the profound aspects of this power:

1. Redemption: The blood of Jesus redeems us from the bondage of sin and the clutches of darkness. It purchases our freedom and secures our place in God's kingdom.

2. Cleansing: It cleanses us from all unrighteousness. Just as physical blood carries impurities away from the body, the blood of Jesus purifies our souls from the stains of sin.

3. Protection: The blood serves as a protective shield, warding off the attacks of the enemy. When we apply the blood in prayer, we invoke divine protection over our lives and loved ones.

4. Healing: The blood of Jesus is not only for the forgiveness of sins but also for physical and emotional healing. It brings restoration to every area of our lives.

5. Access to God: Through the blood, we gain direct access to the throne room of God. We can boldly approach Him, knowing that we are covered by the blood of the Lamb.

Activating the Bloodline Covenant in Midnight Warfare

Midnight warriors must understand the significance of the Bloodline Covenant in their spiritual battles. It is not a distant theological concept but a tangible source of power that can be harnessed to disrupt the activities of darkness. Here's how you can activate the covenant in your midnight warfare:

1. Declare Your Covenant Identity: Begin your prayers by declaring your identity as a blood-bought child of God. Acknowledge that the blood of Jesus flows through your spiritual veins, making you an heir to the covenant promises.

2. Seal Your Territory with the Blood: In spiritual warfare, mark your territory with the blood of Jesus. Speak aloud that no power of darkness can trespass into your life, family, or circumstances because of the protective barrier created by the blood.

3. Plead the Blood: When facing intense spiritual battles, plead the blood of Jesus as your defense. Declare that the enemy has no legal rights over you because you are covered by the blood.

4. Break Curses and Bondages: The blood has the power to break generational curses and bondages. Use it to sever any unholy ties or influences that may have been passed down through your family line.

5. Release Divine Authority: As a midnight warrior, you have been entrusted with the authority to enforce the victory of the cross. By applying the blood, you release this authority over your life and situations.

6. Intercede for Others: Extend the benefits of the Bloodline Covenant to others through intercessory prayer. Pray for the salvation, healing, and deliverance of loved ones, covering them with the blood of Jesus.

7. Celebrate Communion: Regularly partake in communion as a tangible reminder of the covenant. As you partake of the bread and wine, meditate on the significance of Christ's sacrifice and renew your commitment to the covenant.

Your Eternal Legacy

The Bloodline Covenant is not a passive doctrine but an active, life-transforming reality. By embracing its power and applying it in your midnight warfare, you secure not only victory in the present but also your eternal legacy. It is through the blood of Jesus that your name is etched in the annals of heaven, and your legacy as a victorious warrior for Christ is secured.

As you engage in spiritual warfare at the midnight hour, remember that the Bloodline Covenant is your most potent weapon. It is the crimson thread that connects you to the heart of God and ensures that your legacy shines brightly in the eternal tapestry of His kingdom. Embrace it, wield it, and watch as the powers of darkness are disrupted, and your legacy as a Midnight Warrior for Christ is firmly established.

Warfare Prayer

1. In the name of Jesus, I declare that I am a child of the Bloodline Covenant, and my legacy is secured in Christ.

2. By the power of the precious blood of Jesus, I break every generational curse and bondage that has hindered my legacy.

3. I plead the blood of Jesus over my life, family, and circumstances, creating an impenetrable barrier against the enemy's schemes.

4. I declare that the blood of Jesus redeems me from all sin and iniquity, and I am washed clean in His sight.

5. By the authority of the Bloodline Covenant, I release divine healing and restoration into every area of my life.

6. I take authority over every demonic influence and declare that I am free in Jesus' name.

7. In the name of Jesus, I command every power of darkness to flee from my presence, for I am covered by the blood.

8. I declare that the blood of Jesus protects me from all harm and danger, and no weapon formed against me shall prosper.

9. By the blood of the Lamb, I have access to the throne room of God, and I boldly approach His presence with confidence.

10. I speak life and blessing into my legacy, for the blood of Jesus speaks a better word over my life.

11. I break every chain and shackle that has bound my family line, declaring freedom in Jesus' name.

12. I declare that the blood of Jesus is my refuge and fortress, and I dwell securely in Him.

13. By the authority of the Bloodline Covenant, I release the power of the Holy Spirit to empower me in spiritual warfare.

14. I plead the blood of Jesus over my mind, emotions, and thoughts, casting down every stronghold.

15. In Jesus' name, I release the fire of God to consume every work of darkness that has hindered my legacy.

16. I declare that the blood of Jesus covers my loved ones, and they are kept safe from all harm.

17. By the power of the blood, I dismantle every evil altar and demonic stronghold in my life.

18. I decree that the blood of Jesus breaks every yoke of bondage and oppression.

19. I plead the blood over my dreams and visions, that they may be aligned with God's divine purpose for my legacy.

20. In the name of Jesus, I renounce every unholy alliance and covenant, and I am bound only to the Bloodline Covenant.

21. I declare that I am more than a conqueror through Christ Jesus, and no challenge can overcome me.

22. By the blood of Jesus, I release supernatural provision and abundance into my legacy.

23. I take authority over sickness and infirmity, commanding them to leave my body and my family in Jesus' name.

24. I declare that the blood of Jesus seals my territory, and no evil can prevail against me.

25. In Jesus' name, I speak blessings upon the generations to come, that they may walk in the legacy of faith.

26. By the power of the Bloodline Covenant, I release the angels of God to encamp around me and my loved ones.

27. I plead the blood over my words and declarations, that they may carry divine authority and impact.

28. In the name of Jesus, I declare that my legacy will shine as a beacon of light in a dark world.

29. I break every assignment of the enemy to steal, kill, or destroy my legacy, for I am covered by the blood.

30. By the blood of Jesus, I release the gifts and talents that God has placed within me for His glory.

31. I declare that the blood of Jesus transforms me from glory to glory, and I reflect His image in my legacy.

32. In Jesus' name, I command every demonic hindrance to my destiny to be removed, for I am a child of the Bloodline Covenant.

33. I plead the blood over my relationships, that they may be marked by love, unity, and forgiveness.

34. By the authority of the Bloodline Covenant, I declare victory in every spiritual battle I face.

35. I declare that the blood of Jesus covers my past, present, and future, and I walk in divine favor.

36. In the name of Jesus, I release the anointing of the Holy Spirit to break every yoke and release captives.

37. I plead the blood over my decisions and choices, that they may align with God's perfect will for my legacy.

38. By the power of the Bloodline Covenant, I release the blessings of Abraham upon my life and family.

39. I declare that my legacy is a testimony of God's grace, and His glory shines through it.

40. In Jesus' name, I seal these declarations with the blood of the Lamb, and I walk in the authority of the Bloodline Covenant to secure my legacy for generations to come. Amen!

Chapter 23

Heavenly Downloads:
Wisdom for Midnight Warriors

In the dark of the midnight hour, when the world sleeps and the realm of the supernatural awakens, the faithful Midnight Warrior seeks not only to confront the powers of darkness but also to receive divine wisdom. This wisdom is the key that unlocks the mysteries of the spiritual realm, enabling us to navigate the treacherous waters of spiritual warfare with clarity, precision, and unwavering faith. In this chapter, we delve deep into the concept of "Heavenly Downloads," exploring how God imparts His wisdom to those who earnestly seek it.

The Source of Heavenly Downloads

To understand the nature of heavenly downloads, we must first recognize the source from which they flow. God, the Creator of the universe, is the ultimate wellspring of all wisdom. As the book of James reminds us, "If any of you lacks wisdom, let him ask God, who gives generously to all without reproach, and it will be given him" (James 1:5, ESV). In the context of midnight warfare, wisdom becomes our spiritual radar, guiding us through the darkness and revealing the enemy's schemes.

The Midnight Connection

Why is the midnight hour so significant in receiving heavenly downloads? The midnight hour holds a special place in the spiritual realm. It is a time when distractions wane, and the world around us falls into slumber. In this stillness, our hearts and minds are more attuned to the voice of God. Throughout the Bible, we see numerous instances where God chose the midnight hour to communicate His wisdom.

1. Paul and Silas in Prison: Acts 16 recounts the story of Paul and Silas imprisoned in Philippi. At midnight, as they prayed and worshiped, an earthquake shook the prison, setting them free. This midnight encounter with God's power and guidance exemplifies the significance of seeking divine wisdom in the darkest hours.

2. Jacob's Wrestling with God: In Genesis 32, Jacob wrestled with a divine being throughout the night. At daybreak, he received both a new name (Israel) and divine blessings. This event demonstrates the transformative power of seeking God's wisdom through persistent midnight prayer.

3. The Parable of the Ten Virgins: In Matthew 25, Jesus shared the parable of the ten virgins waiting for the bridegroom. The wise virgins, who had enough oil for their lamps, were prepared for his arrival at midnight. They symbolize those who are vigilant and ready to receive God's wisdom when it is most needed.

Preparing for a Heavenly Download

Receiving heavenly downloads isn't a passive process; it requires preparation and intentionality. Here are some key steps to prepare for this divine wisdom:

1. A Surrendered Heart

Before seeking wisdom, it's essential to surrender your heart to God. A heart yielded to His will is more receptive to His guidance.

2. Fervent Prayer

Midnight Warriors should engage in fervent, heartfelt prayer. Praying in the Spirit, with groanings too deep for words (Romans 8:26), can open a conduit for heavenly downloads.

3. Worship and Praise

Just as Paul and Silas worshiped in their prison cell, worship and praise create an atmosphere where God's presence is magnified. Singing psalms, hymns, and spiritual songs can usher in God's wisdom.

4. Meditation on Scripture

Immerse yourself in God's Word. The Bible is a treasure trove of wisdom. Meditate on scripture passages that pertain to your battle and seek understanding from them.

5. Expectation and Faith

Approach the midnight hour with an expectation of God's revelation. Faith is the bridge that connects our hearts to the heavenly realm.

Types of Heavenly Downloads

Heavenly downloads can take various forms, each tailored to your unique spiritual journey. Here are a few common ways in which God imparts His wisdom:

1. Dreams and Visions

God often communicates through dreams and visions. In the Bible, we see Joseph interpreting Pharaoh's dreams and Peter's vision on the rooftop. Pay attention to the symbolism and messages within your dreams.

2. Inner Impressions

Sometimes, God speaks through an inner impression or a "knowing" in your spirit. This can manifest as a sudden clarity of thought or a strong conviction about a course of action.

3. Prophetic Words

God may use prophetic individuals to deliver His wisdom. Be open to receiving guidance from trusted prophets or prophetic words spoken into your life.

4. Scripture Illumination

During your midnight prayer, specific verses may come alive and provide insight into your situation. The Holy Spirit can illuminate scripture to address your needs.

Discerning Heavenly Downloads

Not all thoughts, dreams, or impressions are heavenly downloads. Discernment is crucial to distinguish God's wisdom from other influences. Here are some guidelines:

1. Alignment with Scripture: Any heavenly download should align with the principles and teachings of God's Word.

2. Peace and Confirmation: God's wisdom often comes with a sense of peace and confirmation in your spirit.

3. Confirmation from Others: Seek confirmation from trusted spiritual mentors or fellow believers.

4. Fruitfulness: God's wisdom bears fruit in your life and aligns with His purposes.

Applying Heavenly Wisdom in Midnight Warfare

Once you've received heavenly wisdom, it's essential to apply it effectively in your spiritual warfare. Wisdom equips you with insight into the enemy's tactics, reveals strategic prayer points, and empowers you to claim victory in Jesus' name.

Heavenly downloads are a priceless gift from God, specifically tailored to guide and empower Midnight Warriors in their battles against the forces of darkness. Seek God's wisdom earnestly, prepare your heart and spirit, and remain vigilant during the midnight hour, for in that sacred time, divine wisdom flows like a river, lighting your path and leading you to triumphant victory in Christ.

Warfare Prayer

1. In the mighty name of Jesus, I declare that I am a Midnight Warrior, equipped with divine wisdom to overcome every power of darkness.

2. Heavenly Father, I come before your throne, seeking heavenly downloads of wisdom for my midnight battles. I declare my heart is open to receive your guidance.

3. By the authority of Jesus Christ, I rebuke all confusion and doubt in my mind. I declare a clarity of thought and understanding as I seek your wisdom.

4. I decree that the midnight hour is a sacred time of divine revelation for me. I am alert, prepared, and expectant for heavenly downloads.

5. In Jesus' name, I declare that my prayers in the midnight hour are powerful and effective, piercing through the darkness and dismantling the enemy's plans.

6. Heavenly Father, I declare that I am surrendered to your will, and my heart is yielded to your wisdom. Lead me, guide me, and direct my steps.

7. I decree that as I worship and praise you in the midnight hour, your presence fills the atmosphere, and heavenly downloads flow abundantly.

8. By the blood of Jesus, I declare that I am protected from all spiritual attacks and interference as I seek Your wisdom.

9. I command every stronghold of darkness to crumble before the wisdom of God that is within me. I am an overcomer in Christ Jesus.

10. In Jesus' name, I bind and rebuke all deceptive spirits that seek to distort the heavenly downloads I receive. I declare discernment and clarity.

11. I decree that I am a vigilant Midnight Warrior, watchful and discerning in the spirit. I will not be caught off guard by the enemy's schemes.

12. Heavenly Father, I thank you for the dreams and visions you send in the midnight hour. I declare they are messages of divine wisdom for my journey.

13. In Jesus' name, I decree that I have the mind of Christ, and His wisdom guides my decisions and actions in all areas of my life.

14. I declare that as I meditate on your Word, it becomes a lamp unto my feet and a light unto my path, illuminating the way in my midnight battles.

15. By the authority of Jesus, I declare that I am filled with the Holy Spirit, who reveals hidden truths and imparts heavenly downloads to me.

16. I rebuke fear and anxiety in Jesus' name. I declare a supernatural peace that surpasses all understanding as I receive heavenly wisdom.

17. I command every hindrance and obstacle to the flow of heavenly downloads to be removed in Jesus' name. I am positioned to receive without hindrance.

18. I decree that I am anointed for the midnight hour, and my prayers release divine power to disrupt the activities of darkness.

19. In the name of Jesus, I declare that I walk in the fullness of God's wisdom, and I am a beacon of light in a world of darkness.

20. I thank you, Lord, for the prophetic words spoken into my life. I declare they are arrows of divine wisdom that hit their mark.

21. I declare that every heavenly download I receive bears fruit in my life and aligns with God's purposes for me and my Midnight Warrior journey.

22. In Jesus' name, I bind and cast out all spirits of confusion and deception. I declare a sound mind and discerning spirit.

23. I decree that my thoughts are aligned with the thoughts of Christ. I take every thought captive to the obedience of Christ's wisdom.

24. I declare that as I engage in midnight warfare, the wisdom of God empowers me to see the enemy's strategies and dismantle them.

25. Heavenly Father, I thank you for the wisdom that flows from your throne to guide and protect me in every battle I face.

26. In Jesus' name, I decree that I am not alone in my midnight battles. The angels of God surround me, heeding the wisdom of the Most High.

27. I command every cycle of defeat in my life to be broken by the divine wisdom of God. I am an overcomer through Him who strengthens me.

28. I declare that the wisdom of God brings restoration and healing to every area of my life that has been affected by the enemy's attacks.

29. By the authority of Jesus, I bind and rebuke every spirit of stagnation and delay. I declare a divine acceleration in my journey of faith.

30. I decree that my worship and praise create an atmosphere where God's wisdom is magnified, and His presence is manifest in mighty ways.

31. In Jesus' name, I declare that the heavenly downloads I receive are timely and strategic, enabling me to advance God's kingdom in the darkest places.

32. I rebuke every spirit of fear that seeks to paralyze me in my midnight battles. I declare courage and boldness in the face of adversity.

33. I command every assignment of the enemy against my life to be exposed and nullified by the wisdom of God.

34. I decree that I am a vessel of divine revelation, and the wisdom I receive in the midnight hour flows like a river, refreshing and renewing my spirit.

35. By the authority of Jesus, I break every generational curse and pattern of defeat in my bloodline. I walk in the wisdom of God's Word.

36. I declare that as I present my case before the midnight courts of heaven, divine justice and wisdom prevail on my behalf.

37. In Jesus' name, I declare that the wisdom of God empowers me to discern the times and seasons and align my prayers with His divine agenda.

38. I rebuke every spirit of complacency and apathy. I am a fervent Midnight Warrior, passionate in my pursuit of heavenly wisdom.

39. I command the gates of heaven to open wide, releasing an overflow of heavenly downloads into my life and ministry.

40. In the name of Jesus, I seal these declarations with faith and expectation, knowing that the wisdom of God guides my every step as a Midnight Warrior. Amen.

Chapter 24

Fearless Declarations:
Defying Darkness with Faith

In the darkest hour of the night, when the world is still and shadows loom large, there exists an extraordinary power within the Christian warrior. It's a power that transcends the physical realm and taps into the very heart of the spiritual battle. This power is none other than the fearless declarations of faith, and in this chapter, we will delve deep into its profound significance and how it can be harnessed to defy the darkness that seeks to engulf us.

The Power of Spoken Words

From the very beginning of creation, the power of spoken words has been evident. In Genesis 1, God spoke the universe into existence, declaring, "Let there be light," and there was light. This sets a profound precedent: words have creative power. In the realm of spiritual warfare, our words are not mere utterances; they are weapons, infused with divine authority.

When we declare God's promises, we align ourselves with His divine will. Every word spoken in faith becomes a force to be reckoned with in the spiritual realm. Just as Jesus spoke to the fig tree, and it withered (Matthew 21:19), our declarations can cause the works of darkness to wither and die.

The Anatomy of Fearless Declarations

1. Rooted in Scripture: Fearless declarations must be firmly rooted in the Word of God. It's not about wishful thinking but about declaring God's promises and truths over our lives. For example, declaring, "I am more than a conqueror through Christ who loves me" (Romans 8:37) is a powerful affirmation of our identity in Christ.

2. Specific and Targeted: Vague declarations lack the precision needed for effective warfare. Identify the areas in your life or the lives of those you intercede for that need breakthrough. Specificity in declarations brings clarity and focus.

3. Confident and Bold: Fearlessness is the key. When you declare, do it with unwavering confidence. Remember, doubt is the enemy of faith. Boldly declare God's promises, knowing that He is faithful to fulfill them.

4. Continuous and Consistent: Consistency is crucial in spiritual warfare. Make declarations a daily practice, especially during the midnight hours when the spiritual realm is often more active. The persistence of your declarations wears down the resistance of the enemy.

5. In Alignment with God's Will: Always ensure that your declarations align with God's will. Pray for discernment to understand His plan for your life and declare accordingly.

The Battle for Your Mind

The enemy's primary battleground is the mind. He seeks to plant seeds of doubt, fear, and unbelief. Fearless declarations serve as a defense against these attacks. By consistently speaking God's truth over your mind, you fortify it against the lies of the enemy.

Declare affirmations such as:
- "I have the mind of Christ" (1 Corinthians 2:16).
- "I take every thought captive to the obedience of Christ" (2 Corinthians 10:5).
- "God has not given me a spirit of fear, but of power, love, and a sound mind" (2 Timothy 1:7).

Declarations of Protection

In a world filled with uncertainty and danger, we can declare God's protection over ourselves, our loved ones, and our homes. The midnight hours, often associated with increased spiritual activity, are an opportune time for such declarations.

- "The Lord is my fortress and my deliverer; I will not fear" (Psalm 91:2).

- "No weapon formed against me shall prosper" (Isaiah 54:17).
- "The angel of the Lord encamps around those who fear Him" (Psalm 34:7).

Declarations of Victory

The battle may rage on, but the outcome is already determined. We are on the winning side, and our declarations should reflect this truth.

- "Thanks be to God, who gives us the victory through our Lord Jesus Christ" (1 Corinthians 15:57).
- "In all these things, we are more than conquerors through Him who loved us" (Romans 8:37).
- "The Lord will fight for me; I need only to be still" (Exodus 14:14).

Declarations of Restoration

For those who have faced trials, setbacks, or spiritual attacks, declarations of restoration can be a source of hope and healing.

- "The God of all grace will restore, confirm, strengthen, and establish me" (1 Peter 5:10).
- "I will restore to you the years that the swarming locust has eaten" (Joel 2:25).
- "The Lord heals the brokenhearted and binds up their wounds" (Psalm 147:3).

Declarations of Purpose

Discovering and fulfilling our God-given purpose is a fundamental aspect of our Christian journey. Fearless declarations can help us align with God's calling on our lives.

- "I am fearfully and wonderfully made; God's purpose for me is perfect" (Psalm 139:14).
- "I am created in Christ Jesus for good works, which God prepared beforehand, that I should walk in them" (Ephesians 2:10).
- "I can do all things through Christ who strengthens me" (Philippians 4:13).

The Impact of Fearless Declarations

The impact of fearless declarations goes beyond personal transformation. It ripples through the spiritual realm, disrupting the plans of darkness. As you consistently declare God's truth and promises, you contribute to the advancement of God's kingdom and the defeat of the enemy's schemes.

Fearless declarations are not mere words; they are weapons of spiritual warfare. When spoken in faith, they unleash the power of God into your life and the lives of those you intercede for. Embrace the midnight hour as a time to boldly declare God's truth, defying darkness with unwavering faith. Through fearless declarations, you step into your role as a Midnight Warrior, equipped to overcome the powers of darkness and disrupt their activities.

Warfare Prayer

1. In the mighty name of Jesus, I declare that I am a fearless warrior, unshaken by the darkness that surrounds me.

2. By the authority given to me in Christ, I boldly speak God's promises over my life, knowing that His Word is unshakable.

3. I declare that my words have creative power, just as God's words did at the dawn of creation.

4. In Jesus' name, I speak forth blessings, favor, and divine protection into every area of my life.

5. I declare that I am rooted in the Word of God, and my declarations are firmly anchored in His truth.

6. By the power of Christ within me, I declare specific breakthroughs in areas where I've been facing resistance.

7. I boldly proclaim that doubt and fear have no place in my life; I walk in unwavering confidence in Christ.

8. I declare that I am consistent in my declarations, and I persistently wear down the resistance of the enemy.

9. In alignment with God's will, I declare His plans and purposes over my life and the lives of my loved ones.

10. I take authority over every thought of doubt and fear and declare that my mind is a fortress of faith.

11. By the blood of Jesus, I command every lying spirit to be silenced; I declare God's truth and reject the enemy's lies.

12. I declare protection over my home, that it is a sanctuary of peace and safety in Jesus' name.

13. In the authority of Christ, I command every weapon formed against me to be rendered powerless and ineffective.

14. I declare that I am surrounded by the angelic hosts, and they encamp around me, guarding and protecting me.

15. I take authority over every spiritual attack and declare that no weapon formed against me shall prosper.

16. By faith, I declare victory over every battle and trial; I am more than a conqueror through Christ.

17. I declare that I am an overcomer, and I stand firm in the face of adversity, knowing that God fights for me.

18. I release declarations of healing and restoration into every area of my life and the lives of those in need.

19. I declare that the years lost to the enemy's schemes are being restored to me, a hundredfold.

20. By the power of Christ, I declare that broken hearts are healed, wounds are bound up, and chains are broken.

21. I declare that my purpose in Christ is clear, and I walk in the good works God has prepared for me.

22. I am fearfully and wonderfully made, and I embrace God's perfect purpose for my life.

23. I declare that I can do all things through Christ who strengthens me, and no challenge is too great.

24. I release declarations of divine guidance and wisdom, knowing that God's plans for me are perfect.

25. I declare that my life is a testimony of God's goodness and faithfulness, shining His light in the darkness.

26. I take authority over every spiritual stronghold and declare that they crumble before the name of Jesus.

27. I declare that my worship is a weapon, and as I lift my voice, the enemy flees in fear.

28. By the authority of Christ, I release declarations of revival and awakening in my life and in the world.

29. I declare that my family is covered by the blood of Jesus, and no harm shall befall them.

30. I take authority over generational curses and declare that they are broken in Jesus' name.

31. I declare that my prayers are powerful and effective, shaking the spiritual realm and bringing forth God's will.

32. By faith, I declare that I am a vessel of God's love, bringing hope and healing to those in darkness.

33. I take authority over every storm in my life and declare peace in Jesus' name.

34. I declare that the chains of addiction are broken, and I walk in freedom and victory.

35. I release declarations of unity and harmony in my relationships, knowing that love conquers all.

36. By the authority of Christ, I declare that I am a light in the world, shining brightly in the darkest places.

37. I take authority over every sickness and disease and declare divine health in Jesus' name.

38. I declare that my faith is unshakable, and I stand firm in the promises of God.

39. By the blood of Jesus, I declare that I am cleansed, redeemed, and made righteous.

40. I release declarations of gratitude and thanksgiving, for in all things, I am more than a conqueror through Him who loves me.

Chapter 25

Demons Tremble:
Exercising Authority in Christ

In the dark recesses of the spiritual realm, where the powers of darkness lurk, a truth that sends shudders through the enemy's ranks prevails: demons tremble when confronted by those who understand and wield the authority granted by Christ. As midnight warriors, it is our divine birthright and calling to exercise this authority in the spiritual warfare arena. In this chapter, we delve deep into the biblical foundation, principles, and practical application of this authority, unveiling the mysteries of how demons tremble in the presence of a believer who knows their identity in Christ.

The Source of Our Authority

To grasp the magnitude of our authority in Christ, we must first recognize its source. Our authority doesn't emanate from our own strength or merit; it flows from the throne of God. Jesus Himself declared in Matthew 28:18, "All authority in heaven and on earth has been given to me." As followers of Christ, we share in this authority by virtue of our union with Him. It is an authority that transcends the natural realm, reaching into the spiritual dimensions where battles are waged unseen.

Understanding Our Identity in Christ

Before we can effectively exercise our authority, we must fully understand our identity in Christ. We are not mere mortals engaged in spiritual warfare; we are children of the Most High God, heirs of His kingdom, and co-laborers with Christ. This identity carries with it the weight of authority and the responsibility to steward it wisely.

Ephesians 2:6 reminds us that we have been "raised up with [Christ] and seated with him in the heavenly places." This positioning signifies that we are not bound by earthly limitations but have access to the spiritual realms where principalities and powers operate. Demons tremble at the realization that we are no longer under their dominion but seated in authority over them.

The Weapon of the Word

One of the most potent tools for exercising authority is the Word of God. Hebrews 4:12 tells us that the Word is "sharper than any two-edged sword." When we speak God's Word in faith, it releases spiritual power that causes demons to tremble. Just as Jesus wielded Scripture to rebuke Satan in the wilderness (Matthew 4:1-11), we can use the Word to resist the enemy's advances.

To maximize the impact of God's Word in spiritual warfare, we must immerse ourselves in Scripture, allowing it to dwell richly within us (Colossians 3:16). This not only equips us with a vast arsenal of verses to declare but also fosters an intimate connection with the Word, making it a living, breathing force in our lives.

Praying with Authority

Prayer is another key avenue through which we exercise authority in Christ. When we pray, we are not merely making requests; we are issuing divine decrees and declarations that align with God's will. Our prayers have the power to bind and loose in the spiritual realm (Matthew 18:18), causing demons to tremble as they recognize the authority behind our petitions.

In James 5:16, we are reminded that "the prayer of a righteous person has great power as it is working." Righteousness, attained through faith in Christ, amplifies our authority in prayer. As midnight warriors, our prayers should be bold, targeted, and infused with faith, leaving no room for doubt or fear.

Walking in Holiness

A critical aspect of exercising authority in Christ is maintaining a lifestyle of holiness. Demons tremble when they encounter believers who live in a state of consecration to God. 1 Peter 1:16 instructs us to be holy because God is holy, emphasizing the importance of purity and sanctification.

Holiness is like a radiant light that exposes and dispels the darkness. When we walk in holiness, demons find it increasingly difficult to operate in our presence. Our commitment to purity not only strengthens our authority but also safeguards us from the enemy's snares.

Unity and Corporate Authority

While individual authority is formidable, the power of unity among believers amplifies our impact in the spiritual realm. Jesus promised in Matthew 18:20, "For where two or three are gathered in my name, there am I among them." When we come together in agreement, our authority is exponentially increased, and demons tremble at the collective force of believers in harmony.

Exercising Authority in Deliverance

One of the most direct encounters with demonic forces is in the ministry of deliverance. In this vital aspect of spiritual warfare, we confront demons head-on to set the captives free. Our authority in Christ takes center stage as we command unclean spirits to leave in Jesus' name.

It's crucial to approach deliverance with wisdom, discernment, and prayer. Demons may manifest, resist, or attempt to deceive, but our unwavering confidence in the authority of Christ empowers us to see victory in these confrontations.

Walking in Victory

As midnight warriors, we must continually exercise our authority in Christ with unwavering faith, understanding our identity, and wielding the Word and prayer as powerful weapons. Demons tremble not because of our might but because of the One whose authority we represent. As we walk in holiness, unity, and deliverance, we demonstrate the triumph of Christ over the powers of darkness, bringing glory to His name and ushering in the kingdom of light. Let us go forth, armed with authority, to disrupt the activities of the enemy and advance the cause of Christ in the midnight hour.

Warfare Prayer

1. In the name of Jesus, I declare that I am a child of the Most High God, seated in heavenly places with Christ.

2. By the authority of Jesus, I rebuke all powers of darkness that seek to hinder my walk with God.

3. I declare that the Word of God is a two-edged sword in my mouth, cutting through every demonic scheme.

4. In Jesus' name, I command every demon to tremble and flee as I speak the truth of God's Word.

5. I exercise my authority in Christ to bind every spirit of fear, doubt, and unbelief in my life.

6. By the power of the Holy Spirit, I decree victory over every spiritual battle I face.

7. I declare that the blood of Jesus covers me, protecting me from all evil influences.

8. In Jesus' name, I break every chain and shackle that the enemy has placed upon my life.

9. I take authority over the spirits of confusion and deception, releasing clarity and discernment.

10. By the authority of Christ, I command every demon assigned against my family to flee.

11. I declare that my prayers are powerful and effective in the realm of the spirit.

12. In the name of Jesus, I bind the strongholds of addiction and bondage in my life and the lives of my loved ones.

13. I decree that I am a vessel of God's glory, and darkness cannot prevail against me.

14. By the authority of Jesus, I release the fire of the Holy Spirit to consume every work of the enemy.

15. I declare that angels are encamped around me, guarding me from all harm.

16. In Jesus' name, I renounce all generational curses and declare the blessings of Christ over my bloodline.

17. I exercise my authority to bring healing and restoration to every area of my life.

18. By the power of Christ, I declare that I am more than a conqueror through Him who loves me.

19. I take authority over every storm in my life, commanding peace and stillness in Jesus' name.

20. In Jesus' name, I release the anointing of the Holy Spirit to destroy yokes and burdens.

21. I declare that my worship is a weapon, and I will praise God in the midst of the battle.

22. By the authority of Christ, I bind the spirit of division and release unity in my relationships and church.

23. I decree that every demonic assignment against my purpose and destiny is canceled.

24. In Jesus' name, I take authority over sickness and disease, declaring divine health.

25. I exercise my authority to pray for the nations, asking for God's mercy and revival.

26. By the power of Christ, I command every demonic assignment against my dreams and visions to be broken.

27. I declare that I am a temple of the Holy Spirit, and darkness has no place in me.

28. In Jesus' name, I release supernatural provision and abundance in every area of my life.

29. I take authority over the spirit of hopelessness and release a spirit of hope and expectation.

30. By the authority of Christ, I bind every spirit of rejection and declare that I am accepted in the beloved.

31. I decree that the enemy's plans to steal, kill, and destroy in my life are thwarted in Jesus' name.

32. In the name of Jesus, I command every demonic stronghold to crumble and be replaced with the kingdom of God.

33. I exercise my authority to pray for the lost, declaring that they will come to know Christ.

34. By the power of Christ, I release the peace of God that surpasses all understanding into my circumstances.

35. I declare that I am a warrior in God's army, and I will not be defeated by the enemy.

36. In Jesus' name, I take authority over every storm in my life, speaking calmness and tranquility.

37. I decree that the light of Christ shines brightly in me, dispelling all darkness.

38. By the authority of Christ, I bind every spirit of despair and release a spirit of joy and rejoicing.

39. I exercise my authority to pray for divine appointments and opportunities to share the gospel.

40. In the name of Jesus, I declare that I am an overcomer, and no weapon formed against me shall prosper.

Chapter 26

Midnight Healing:
Prayers for Divine Restoration

In the darkest hours of the night, when the world sleeps, and the stillness of the midnight hour surrounds you, there lies a profound opportunity for healing and restoration. Midnight is a sacred time, a time when the veils between the natural and the supernatural are thinner, and the divine presence is keenly felt. In this chapter, we delve deep into the concept of Midnight Healing—a spiritual phenomenon that transcends the boundaries of time and space, ushering in divine restoration in our lives.

The Midnight Hour: A Divine Appointment

The concept of Midnight Healing is rooted in the biblical narrative. In the book of Acts, we read about the Apostle Paul and Silas, who found themselves imprisoned in the depths of a dark jail cell. It was at midnight, in the midst of their suffering, that they turned to prayer and worship. As they praised God, a supernatural earthquake shook the foundations of the prison, and their chains fell off. This dramatic event serves as a powerful testament to the potential for divine intervention during the midnight hour.

Midnight is not just a time on the clock; it symbolizes the darkest moments in our lives. It represents our trials, afflictions, and challenges. It is in these moments that we can turn to God for healing and restoration. The midnight hour becomes a divine appointment with the Creator, a time when heaven touches earth.

Understanding Divine Restoration

Divine restoration is a multifaceted concept that encompasses healing, renewal, and the rebuilding of what has been broken or lost. It is a process in which God, in His infinite mercy and love, brings back to us that which the enemy has stolen or that which life's trials have taken away. It is a promise of hope in the midst of despair.

Restoration can take many forms:

1. Physical Healing: Midnight Healing often involves prayers for physical ailments. Whether you are battling illness, disease, or injury, the midnight hour is a potent time to seek divine intervention for your health.

2. Emotional Healing: The scars of emotional wounds can run deep. In the midnight hour, you can pour out your heart to God, seeking healing from past traumas, anxiety, depression, or grief.

3. Relational Healing: Broken relationships can be one of life's most painful experiences. Midnight prayers can be directed towards restoring fractured relationships with family, friends, or loved ones.

4. Financial Restoration: In times of financial hardship, the midnight hour is a time to petition God for financial breakthroughs, debt relief, and abundance.

5. Spiritual Renewal: If you've strayed from your faith or feel spiritually depleted, Midnight Healing can bring a profound renewal of your relationship with God.

Prayers for Divine Restoration

Midnight Healing is not just about asking God for restoration; it's about engaging in powerful, faith-filled prayers that align with His promises. Here are some prayer points for Midnight Healing:

1. Prayer of Surrender

Begin by surrendering your burdens and wounds to God. Acknowledge your need for His healing touch. Psalm 34:18 reminds us that "The Lord is close to the brokenhearted and saves those who are crushed in spirit."

2. Prayer of Forgiveness

Forgiveness is a crucial step in the healing process. Forgive those who have hurt you, and ask God to forgive any bitterness or resentment in your heart. This prayer aligns with Matthew 6:14-15, where Jesus teaches us about forgiveness.

3. Prayer of Restoration

Pray specifically for the areas in your life where you seek restoration. Use Scriptures like Joel 2:25-26 as a foundation for your prayers: "I will restore to you the years that the swarming locust has eaten... You shall eat in plenty and be satisfied."

4. Prayer of Faith

Exercise faith as you pray. Remember the words of Jesus in Mark 11:24: "Therefore I tell you, whatever you ask in prayer, believe that you have received it, and it will be yours."

5. Prayer of Thanksgiving

Express gratitude to God in advance for His healing and restoration. Thank Him for His promises and for being a God of mercy and grace.

6. Prayer of Declaration

Speak declarations of healing and restoration over your life. Proclaim God's promises boldly, knowing that His Word does not return void (Isaiah 55:11).

The Midnight Healing Experience

The Midnight Healing experience is a deeply personal and intimate one. It involves more than just words; it involves your heart, your faith, and your connection with the divine. As you engage in Midnight Healing, consider the following tips:

1. Find a Quiet Place

Select a quiet, private place where you can focus without distractions. Midnight is a time of stillness, and your surroundings should reflect that.

2. Worship in Song

Just as Paul and Silas worshiped in their prison cell, begin your Midnight Healing session with worship. Sing songs of praise and adoration to God.

3. Meditate on Scripture

Immerse yourself in Scripture that speaks of God's healing and restoration. Verses like Isaiah 61:7 and Jeremiah 30:17 can provide comfort and inspiration.

4. Pour Out Your Heart

Don't hold back in your prayers. Be open and honest with God about your pain, your struggles, and your desires for healing and restoration.

5. Listen for His Voice

In the stillness of the midnight hour, be attentive to God's voice. He may speak to you through impressions, thoughts, or a deep sense of peace.

Midnight Healing is a powerful and transformative practice for those seeking divine restoration. It is a reminder that God is always ready to meet us in our darkest moments and bring healing, renewal, and hope. As you embark on this journey of Midnight Healing, may you experience the profound touch of God's love and the restoration of all that is broken in your life.

Warfare Prayer

1. By the authority of Jesus' name, I declare healing over my body, mind, and spirit.

2. In Jesus' name, I release forgiveness and let go of all bitterness and resentment.

3. I declare that every stolen blessing and opportunity is restored to me in abundance.

4. By the power of Jesus, I command every sickness to leave my body now.

5. I declare that my emotional wounds are healed, and I walk in divine peace.

6. In the name of Jesus, I break every chain of addiction and bondage.

7. I decree that my relationships are restored and filled with love and understanding.

8. By the authority of Jesus' name, I release financial breakthroughs and prosperity into my life.

9. I declare that my faith is renewed, and I walk in unwavering trust in God.

10. In Jesus' name, I receive a fresh anointing of the Holy Spirit for spiritual revival.

11. I command every spirit of fear and anxiety to flee from my life.

12. By the power of Jesus' blood, I am cleansed and made whole.

13. I declare that my family is blessed and protected under the covering of the Lord.

14. In Jesus' name, I speak restoration to every area of brokenness in my life.

15. I decree that I am a conqueror through Christ who strengthens me.

16. By the authority of Jesus, I break the grip of depression and declare joy and peace.

17. I declare that my children are raised in the fear and admonition of the Lord.

18. In Jesus' name, I release financial debt and walk in financial freedom.

19. I command every spiritual attack to cease in Jesus' mighty name.

20. I declare that God's favor surrounds me like a shield.

21. By the authority of Jesus' name, I break generational curses and declare blessings.

22. I decree that I am a vessel of God's love and healing to others.

23. In Jesus' name, I release creativity and divine inspiration into my life.

24. I command every door of opportunity to open in Jesus' name.

25. I declare that I am fearfully and wonderfully made by my Creator.

26. By the authority of Jesus, I declare healing over my loved ones.

27. I decree that I am a warrior of light, dispelling darkness wherever I go.

28. In Jesus' name, I break the power of negative words spoken against me.

29. I command divine restoration in my marriage and family relationships.

30. I declare that I am the head and not the tail, above and not beneath.

31. By the authority of Jesus' name, I am released from the past and step into a new season.

32. I decree that my prayers are powerful and effective, moving mountains.

33. In Jesus' name, I release healing over the nations and pray for peace.

34. I command every hindrance to my destiny to be removed in Jesus' name.

35. I declare that I am a child of God, chosen and dearly loved.

36. By the authority of Jesus, I declare that no weapon formed against me shall prosper.

37. I decree that I am an overcomer, more than a conqueror through Christ.

38. In Jesus' name, I speak life and restoration into every dead situation.

39. I command every spirit of despair to bow before the name of Jesus.

40. I declare that as I pray in the midnight hour, God's healing and restoration flow into my life in abundance.

Chapter 27

Victory in the Valley:
Triumph in Midnight Warfare

In the spiritual realm, the concept of valleys holds profound significance. Throughout the Bible, valleys are often associated with challenges, trials, and moments of testing. Yet, they are also places where incredible victories can be won. In this chapter, we will delve into the depths of the spiritual valleys, exploring the significance of these places and how to achieve triumph through midnight warfare, all from a Christian perspective.

The Symbolism of Valleys

Valleys appear throughout Scripture as locations where God's people faced adversity and opposition. One of the most famous biblical valleys is the Valley of Elah, where David faced the giant Goliath. It was in this valley that the seemingly insurmountable odds against the young shepherd-boy-turned-warrior transformed into a triumphant victory for God's people. Valleys symbolize the battlegrounds where God's power is often most vividly displayed.

The Midnight Warriors' Journey

To understand how to triumph in the valley through midnight warfare, we must first recognize that spiritual valleys are not to be avoided but embraced. Just as David did not shy away from Goliath in the Valley of Elah, we must confront the challenges that come our way. These valleys represent our spiritual battlegrounds, and as midnight warriors, we are called to engage in the fight.

1. Recognizing the Valley: The first step is acknowledging when you are in a spiritual valley. These moments often come when you are facing intense trials, doubt, or spiritual attacks. It's essential to discern when you are in the valley and not mistake it for a permanent dwelling.

2. Seeking Divine Guidance: In the valley, it's crucial to seek divine guidance through prayer and meditation. Ask God for wisdom and insight into the challenges you are facing. Remember, the Lord is your shepherd, even in the valley (Psalm 23:4).

3. Preparation for Battle: Just as David gathered five smooth stones before facing Goliath, prepare yourself for the battle ahead. Equip yourself with the armor of God (Ephesians 6:10-18), and arm yourself with powerful midnight prayers.

4. The Power of Praise: In the valley, praise becomes a potent weapon. When you lift your voice in worship and adoration, you declare God's sovereignty over your circumstances. Like Paul and Silas in the prison (Acts 16:25), your praise can break chains and bring deliverance.

Engaging in Midnight Warfare

Midnight warfare is a specialized form of spiritual battle that occurs during the darkest hours of the night. This is a time when the enemy often seeks to launch his attacks, but it can also be a time when God's power is most accessible.

1. Strategic Prayer Watches: The midnight hours are divided into prayer watches, each with its unique significance. The watch from 12 AM to 3 AM is known as the "Brazen Altar Watch." It's a time to pray for purification and consecration.

2. Binding and Loosing: In Matthew 18:18, Jesus gave us the authority to bind and loose in heaven and on earth. In the valley, use this authority to bind the works of the enemy and release God's blessings and favor over your life.

3. Decrees and Declarations: Speak powerful decrees and declarations into the spiritual atmosphere of the valley. Declare victory, healing, and restoration over your circumstances. Proclaim the promises of God's Word.

4. Intercessory Warfare: Engage in intercessory prayer not only for yourself but for others who may be in the same valley. Your prayers can be a source of strength and hope for those around you.

Triumphing in the Valley

Triumph in the valley is not the absence of challenges but the presence of God's power and grace. It's the assurance that even in the darkest moments, God is working all things together for your good (Romans 8:28).

1. Confidence in God's Promises: Stand firmly on the promises of God. Memorize Scripture verses that speak to your situation and use them as your declaration of faith.

2. Persistence in Prayer: Don't give up. Midnight warriors understand the power of persistence in prayer. Like the persistent widow in Luke 18:1-8, keep knocking on Heaven's door until your breakthrough comes.

3. Community and Support: Seek support from your spiritual community. Share your struggles and victories with fellow believers who can uplift and encourage you in your journey through the valley.

4. Expect Miracles: Midnight warfare often leads to miraculous breakthroughs. Be expectant of God's supernatural intervention in your situation.

The valley is not a place of defeat for the midnight warrior; it's a place of opportunity. It's where you can demonstrate your unwavering faith, persistence in prayer, and reliance on God's power. Embrace the valley as your battlefield, and through midnight warfare, you will not only triumph but also bring glory to God in the darkest of times.

Warfare Prayer

1. In the name of Jesus, I declare that I am a midnight warrior, and the valley is my battleground for triumph.

2. Heavenly Father, I acknowledge the significance of the valleys in my life and declare that they are places of divine opportunity.

3. I thank you, Lord, for your presence with me in every valley, guiding me with your wisdom and light.

4. By the authority of Jesus' name, I bind any spiritual forces of darkness that seek to hinder my victory in the valley.

5. I loose the power of God's Word and promises over my life in the valley, knowing that all things work together for my good.

6. I declare that I am equipped with the full armor of God, ready to face any challenge in the valley.

7. By the blood of Jesus, I am protected and covered from all harm and attacks in the valley.

8. I praise and worship God in the midst of my trials, knowing that my praise breaks chains and releases divine favor.

9. I decree that I walk in divine guidance and discernment in the valley, for the Lord is my Shepherd.

10. In the name of Jesus, I declare that I am prepared for battle, just as David was with his five smooth stones.

11. I decree that my prayers in the midnight hours are strategic and effective, aligning with God's purposes.

12. I bind every spirit of fear and doubt that attempts to paralyze me in the valley.

13. I loose the spirit of faith and courage, knowing that with God, I am more than a conqueror.

14. I declare that the enemy's plans in the valley are thwarted, and his strongholds are demolished.

15. By the authority of Jesus, I release healing and restoration over my life and circumstances.

16. I decree that I am an intercessor in the midnight hours, standing in the gap for others in the valley.

17. In the name of Jesus, I bind the works of darkness and loose the light of God's truth and revelation.

18. I declare that I have the power to bind and loose, according to Matthew 18:18, for God's glory.

19. I decree that I am a watchman on the wall, vigilant and discerning in the midnight hours.

20. I bind every spirit of despair and hopelessness, and I release the spirit of hope and joy.

21. I declare that my praise in the valley releases supernatural breakthroughs and miracles.

22. I loose God's angels to encamp around me and protect me in the valley.

23. I decree that my prayers in the valley are fervent and effectual, producing great results.

24. In the name of Jesus, I bind every demonic assignment against my life and destiny.

25. I declare that I am rooted and grounded in the Word of God, unshaken by the storms of the valley.

26. I loose the peace of God that surpasses all understanding to guard my heart and mind.

27. I decree that I am a overcomer through the blood of Jesus and the word of my testimony.

28. By the authority of Jesus, I rebuke every spirit of confusion and chaos in the valley.

29. I declare that I am a vessel of God's love and grace, bringing light into the darkness of the valley.

30. I bind every hindrance to my spiritual growth and loose the blessings of spiritual maturity.

31. In the name of Jesus, I declare that I am surrounded by a great cloud of witnesses cheering me on in the valley.

32. I decree that the valley is a place of divine encounters, where God's presence is manifest.

33. I bind every generational curse and release the blessings of Abraham over my life.

34. I declare that my prayers in the valley release divine solutions and breakthrough strategies.

35. I loose the fire of the Holy Spirit to burn away every impurity in my life in the valley.

36. By the authority of Jesus, I declare that the valley is a place of promotion and elevation.

37. I decree that I am a living testimony of God's faithfulness and victory in the valley.

38. In the name of Jesus, I bind every hindrance to my destiny and loose divine acceleration.

39. I declare that I am more than a conqueror in Christ Jesus, and I will triumph in the valley.

40. Heavenly Father, I thank you for the ultimate victory I have in Jesus, and I walk in that victory in every valley of my life. Amen.

Chapter 28

Illuminating the Shadows:
Exposing the Enemy's Schemes

In the realm of spiritual warfare, one of the most crucial aspects of victory is the ability to discern and expose the schemes of the enemy. Darkness operates best in secrecy, and it is the duty of the Midnight Warrior to shine the light of divine revelation upon the hidden works of the adversary. In this chapter, we will delve deeply into the strategies and methods for exposing the enemy's schemes with precision and effectiveness.

The Battlefield of the Mind

Before we embark on our journey to unveil the enemy's schemes, it's essential to understand the battleground - the human mind. The enemy often launches his attacks by planting seeds of doubt, fear, and deception in our minds. These are the shadows where his schemes take root and grow. To expose these schemes, we must first recognize and confront them within ourselves.

The Power of Discernment

Discernment is the supernatural ability to perceive the spiritual forces at work behind the scenes. It is a gift from God that enables us to see beyond the natural realm into the spiritual dimension. Midnight Warriors must cultivate discernment through prayer, fasting, and the study of God's Word. As we draw closer to the Lord, our spiritual senses become sharper, allowing us to detect the enemy's presence and schemes.

Unmasking Deception

One of the enemy's primary tactics is deception. He masquerades as an angel of light, seeking to lead believers astray. To expose his deception, we must be firmly grounded in the truth of God's Word. The Bible is our ultimate weapon against lies and falsehoods. By comparing every thought, message, or vision to the Word, we can discern whether it is from God or the enemy.

Strategic Intercession

Prayer is a potent tool for exposing the enemy's schemes. Through strategic intercession, we can petition the Lord for insight into the plans of darkness. Midnight Warriors often engage in focused prayer sessions, asking the Holy Spirit to reveal hidden plots, uncover demonic strongholds, and unveil the enemy's tactics. These prayers not only expose the schemes but also neutralize them.

Spiritual Intelligence

Just as military strategists gather intelligence on their adversaries, so too must we gather spiritual intelligence on the enemy. This involves keeping watch in the spirit realm, being attuned to signs of spiritual warfare, and seeking divine insights. Dreams, visions, and prophetic words can all be sources of valuable intelligence. By collecting and interpreting this information, we gain a clearer understanding of the enemy's plans.

Exposing the Enemy's Agents

The enemy often operates through human agents who unwittingly or willingly carry out his schemes. These agents can be found in various spheres of society, including politics, entertainment, and even within the church. Midnight Warriors must be discerning enough to recognize when someone is being used by the enemy. This discernment enables us to pray for their deliverance and, in some cases, confront them with the truth of Christ.

Spiritual Warfare Mapping

Similar to military intelligence maps, spiritual warfare mapping involves identifying strategic locations and strongholds where the enemy operates. Midnight Warriors create spiritual maps that pinpoint areas of darkness, such as drug-infested neighborhoods, occult practices, or regions plagued by violence. By mapping these areas, we can strategically target them in prayer and spiritual warfare, bringing the light of Christ into the darkest places.

Exposing the Occult

The occult is a breeding ground for the enemy's schemes. It encompasses practices like witchcraft, divination, and sorcery. Midnight Warriors must be equipped to expose and combat these dark arts. This involves researching occult practices, understanding their methodologies, and engaging in prayer and spiritual warfare to dismantle occult strongholds.

Spiritual Counterintelligence

In the world of espionage, counterintelligence seeks to thwart the plans of the enemy. Similarly, in spiritual warfare, we engage in counterintelligence by uncovering the enemy's plots and actively working to disrupt them. This may involve prophetic acts, binding and loosing, or targeted prayer campaigns. Midnight Warriors must be proactive in their efforts to counter the enemy's schemes.

The Authority of the Midnight Warrior

Ultimately, the authority to expose and defeat the enemy's schemes comes from Christ Himself. As Midnight Warriors, we stand on the solid foundation of Jesus' victory on the cross. We have been given the authority to trample on serpents and scorpions and to overcome all the power of the enemy (Luke 10:19). This authority is not based on our strength but on our relationship with the King of Kings.

"Illuminating the Shadows: Exposing the Enemy's Schemes" is a vital chapter in the Midnight Warfare Handbook. It equips believers with the knowledge, discernment, and strategies needed to uncover and thwart the enemy's plans. By shining the light of Christ into the darkest corners of the spiritual realm, we not only protect ourselves but also advance the kingdom of God, reclaiming territory for the glory of the Lord. Remember, as a Midnight Warrior, you are called to be a light in the darkness, exposing the enemy's schemes and ushering in the victory of Christ.

Warfare Prayer

1. In the name of Jesus, I declare that I am a Midnight Warrior, called to expose the enemy's schemes and walk in the light of Christ.

2. By the power of the Holy Spirit, I discern and expose every hidden scheme of the enemy operating in my life and my surroundings.

3. I declare that the battlefield of my mind belongs to the Lord, and I resist all doubt, fear, and deception.

4. In Jesus' name, I decree that the gift of discernment operates strongly in my life, revealing the spiritual forces at work behind the scenes.

5. I declare that I am grounded in the truth of God's Word, and I use it as a weapon to unmask every deception of the enemy.

6. By the authority of Christ, I command every lie and falsehood in my life to be exposed and brought into the light.

7. I declare that my prayers are strategic and powerful, unveiling the enemy's plans and disrupting his activities.

8. In the name of Jesus, I expose and bind every demonic stronghold that seeks to hinder my spiritual progress.

9. I decree that I am watchful in the spirit realm, discerning signs of spiritual warfare and receiving divine insights.

10. By the blood of Jesus, I cover myself and my loved ones, rendering us invisible to the enemy's schemes.

11. I declare that I am a watchman on the wall, alert to the enemy's movements and ready to intercede on behalf of others.

12. In Jesus' name, I expose and dismantle every occult practice and stronghold in my community.

13. I declare that I have the authority to confront and lead individuals trapped in the enemy's deception to the truth of Christ.

14. By the power of the Holy Spirit, I create spiritual warfare maps that target and expose areas of darkness in my region.

15. I decree that the light of Christ shines brightly in every place I step, dispelling darkness and exposing hidden works.

16. In the name of Jesus, I engage in counterintelligence, disrupting the enemy's plans and advancing God's kingdom.

17. I declare that I am clothed in the armor of God, equipped to withstand and expose every scheme of the enemy.

18. By the authority of Christ, I expose and break every curse and generational stronghold in my family.

19. I decree that my prayers are like arrows of light, piercing the darkness and revealing the glory of God.

20. In Jesus' name, I rebuke every spirit of confusion and chaos, and I release divine order and clarity.

21. I declare that I am an ambassador of Christ, representing His kingdom and authority on earth.

22. By the power of the Holy Spirit, I uncover and dismantle every network of darkness operating in my city.

23. I decree that the enemy's plans are exposed and rendered powerless in the face of God's mighty hand.

24. In the name of Jesus, I release the fire of the Holy Spirit to burn away every scheme of the enemy.

25. I declare that I am a vessel of divine intelligence, receiving supernatural insights to thwart the enemy's strategies.

26. By the authority of Christ, I bind every spirit of deception and release a spirit of truth and revelation.

27. I decree that my prayers are effective in uncovering and dismantling the hidden agendas of darkness.

28. In Jesus' name, I expose and confront every false doctrine and heresy that seeks to deceive God's people.

29. I declare that I have the discernment to recognize the schemes of the enemy, even when they are cloaked in disguise.

30. By the power of the Holy Spirit, I release a spirit of repentance and revival that exposes sin and leads to transformation.

31. I decree that the enemy's tactics are futile in the face of God's wisdom and discernment within me.

32. In the name of Jesus, I expose and break every chain of bondage that the enemy has placed on individuals.

33. I declare that I am a vessel of light, illuminating the darkness and guiding others to Christ.

34. By the authority of Christ, I release angels to uncover and thwart the plans of darkness.

35. I decree that the enemy's strategies are revealed and nullified, and God's purposes prevail.

36. In Jesus' name, I declare that I am a spiritual gatekeeper, allowing only that which aligns with God's will to enter.

37. I release the sound of victory, proclaiming that every scheme of the enemy is defeated in Jesus' name.

38. I decree that I am an overcomer, walking in the authority of Christ and exposing the enemy's schemes.

39. By the power of the Holy Spirit, I declare that darkness trembles in the presence of God's light within me.

40. In the name of Jesus, I declare that I am a vessel of revelation and illumination, exposing the enemy's schemes and advancing the kingdom of God. Amen.

Chapter 29

A Legacy of Light:
Passing Down Midnight Warfare

In the realm of spiritual warfare, as with any noble pursuit, the passing down of knowledge and experience from one generation to another is a sacred duty. Just as seasoned warriors train the next generation of soldiers, so too must midnight warriors ensure that the legacy of their spiritual battles endures. In this chapter, we delve deep into the importance of passing down midnight warfare strategies, prayers, and wisdom, rooted in the Christian faith.

The Spiritual Ancestry

Our faith as Christians is deeply rooted in a tradition of passing down wisdom and spiritual insight. We see this in the Old Testament, where the patriarchs and prophets passed down their encounters with God and the lessons learned in their journeys. Abraham passed down his faith to Isaac, who in turn passed it down to Jacob. Moses shared his divine encounters with God, and Elijah mentored Elisha, who asked for a double portion of his mentor's spirit.

Likewise, in the New Testament, we witness the Apostle Paul investing in the spiritual growth of his disciple, Timothy. In 2 Timothy 2:2, Paul instructs Timothy, "And the things you have heard me say in the presence of many witnesses entrust to reliable people who will also be qualified to teach others." This chain of spiritual heritage is a hallmark of our faith, and it extends to the realm of midnight warfare.

The Passing Down of Midnight Wisdom

Midnight warriors are called to be vigilant, discerning, and bold. As you have journeyed through the previous chapters of this handbook, you have learned the potent strategies and prayers that can disrupt the activities of the powers of darkness. Now, the question arises: how do you ensure that this knowledge and power are passed down to future generations of spiritual warriors?

1. Mentorship and Discipleship

One of the most effective ways to pass down midnight warfare knowledge is through mentorship and discipleship. Just as Paul invested in Timothy, seasoned midnight warriors should identify and mentor younger believers who show a passion for spiritual warfare. This mentorship should involve not only teaching but also modeling a life of prayer, faith, and spiritual authority.

2. Family Altars

In many Christian traditions, the concept of a "family altar" is revered. It is a place where families gather for prayer, worship, and the reading of Scripture. It is also an ideal setting to pass down midnight warfare practices. Parents can teach their children the importance of spiritual warfare, share personal testimonies of victories won through prayer, and engage in midnight intercession as a family.

3. Midnight Prayer Watches

Consider establishing a regular midnight prayer watch within your church or community. This is a powerful way to gather believers of all ages and backgrounds to engage in collective warfare against the powers of darkness. Younger members can learn from the experiences and wisdom of their elders during these prayer watches.

4. Written Legacy

In addition to oral instruction and mentorship, consider creating written materials that capture the essence of midnight warfare. This could be in the form of books, manuals, or digital resources. Document the prayers, strategies, and testimonies of victories. Ensure that these resources are accessible to future generations of warriors.

The Importance of Testimonies

Testimonies are potent tools for passing down the legacy of midnight warfare. They not only inspire faith but also provide practical examples of how God intervenes in the battles of life. Encourage those who have experienced breakthroughs through midnight warfare to share their stories. These testimonies serve as beacons of hope and faith for others.

Embracing the Call to Legacy

Passing down the legacy of midnight warfare is not just a duty; it's a sacred calling. As you invest in the spiritual growth of others, you become part of a chain that extends through time and eternity. Your knowledge, prayers, and victories become a light that pierces the darkness for generations to come.

"A Legacy of Light: Passing Down Midnight Warfare" is a vital chapter in the journey of every midnight warrior. It is a call to invest in the spiritual growth of others, to ensure that the knowledge and power acquired in the battles of the night continue to disrupt the activities of the powers of darkness. Embrace this calling with passion and dedication, for you are not just fighting for your generation but for those yet to come. In this way, the legacy of midnight warfare endures, and the light of Christ shines ever brighter in the darkest hours of the night.

Warfare Prayer

1. In the name of Jesus, I declare that I am a guardian of the Legacy of Light, committed to passing down midnight warfare wisdom to the next generation.

2. By the authority of Jesus Christ, I pray for divine discernment to recognize those whom I am called to mentor in the ways of spiritual warfare.

3. I declare that I will not keep the knowledge of midnight warfare to myself but will invest in others for the glory of God.

4. In Jesus' name, I declare that my family will be a strong spiritual lineage, passing down the legacy of midnight prayer and warfare.

5. By the power of the Holy Spirit, I decree that our family altar will be a place of revelation, transformation, and intercession.

6. I take authority over any hindrance that may try to disrupt the passing down of midnight warfare knowledge in my church and community.

7. In the name of Jesus, I declare that I will be a faithful and effective mentor, teaching and modeling the principles of spiritual warfare.

8. I rebuke any spirit of fear or hesitation that may try to hinder me from sharing my personal testimonies of victory in midnight warfare.

9. By the blood of Jesus, I release an anointing for warfare upon the next generation, equipping them to stand boldly against the powers of darkness.

10. I decree that the written legacy of midnight warfare will reach far and wide, impacting countless lives for God's glory.

11. In Jesus' name, I declare that testimonies of midnight breakthroughs will multiply, inspiring faith and hope in the hearts of many.

12. I take authority over any distractions that may try to divert our focus from passing down A Legacy of Light.

13. By the power of Christ, I break any generational curses that may have hindered the legacy of spiritual warfare in my family.

14. I decree that our midnight prayer watches will be powerful and anointed, shaking the foundations of darkness.

15. In the name of Jesus, I declare that the next generation will rise up as mighty warriors, unafraid of spiritual battles.

16. I rebuke any spirit of complacency that may attempt to weaken our commitment to passing down the legacy.

17. By the authority of Christ, I release an impartation of wisdom, discernment, and prophetic insight upon those I mentor.

18. I decree that the resources created to capture the essence of midnight warfare will be impactful and transformational.

19. In Jesus' name, I declare that our testimonies will echo in the spiritual realm, causing confusion and defeat among the enemy's ranks.

20. I take authority over any doubts or insecurities that may try to undermine my role in passing down A Legacy of Light.

21. By the blood of Jesus, I cover the next generation with divine protection as they step into the battlefield of spiritual warfare.

22. I decree that the chain of spiritual heritage will remain unbroken, stretching from generation to generation.

23. In the name of Jesus, I declare that the light of Christ will shine brighter in the darkest hours of the night through our prayers.

24. I rebuke any spirit of division that may try to infiltrate our efforts to pass down the legacy.

25. By the power of Christ, I release an anointing for radical praise and worship in our midnight battles.

26. I decree that supernatural encounters with God will be a hallmark of the next generation of midnight warriors.

27. In Jesus' name, I declare that our family, church, and community will be known as strongholds of prayer and spiritual authority.

28. I take authority over any distractions that may attempt to divert our focus from the importance of legacy.

29. By the authority of Christ, I release a spirit of unity and collaboration among those called to pass down A Legacy of Light.

30. I decree that the testimonies of victories won through midnight warfare will draw multitudes to Christ.

31. In the name of Jesus, I declare that spiritual strongholds will crumble as we pass down the legacy of spiritual warfare.

32. I rebuke any hindrance that may try to hinder the spread of written materials on midnight warfare.

33. By the power of Christ, I release a revival of midnight prayer and intercession in our communities.

34. I decree that the next generation will surpass us in their zeal and effectiveness in midnight warfare.

35. In Jesus' name, I declare that our prayers will be like fire, consuming the works of darkness.

36. I take authority over any spiritual opposition that may rise against those dedicated to passing down the legacy.

37. By the authority of Christ, I release a spirit of courage and boldness upon those who embrace the call to legacy.

38. I decree that our midnight warfare will be marked by signs, wonders, and miraculous interventions.

39. In the name of Jesus, I declare that the legacy of light will endure, shining throughout eternity.

40. I thank you, Lord, for the privilege of being a part of passing down A Legacy of Light, and I commit to this sacred task with unwavering faith and determination. Amen.

Chapter 30

The Midnight Triumph:
Celebrating Your Victories

In the darkness of the midnight hour, you've fought valiantly against the powers of darkness. You've waged spiritual warfare, engaged in violent prayers, and declared decrees that have shaken the very foundations of the enemy's domain. Now, as dawn breaks on the horizon, it's time to turn your attention to a vital aspect of your journey: celebrating your victories.

The Power of Celebration

Celebration is more than just a joyful expression; it's a spiritual weapon. When you celebrate your victories, you're not merely reveling in your success; you're magnifying the glory of God. It's a profound act of gratitude that amplifies the impact of your prayers and decrees.

In the Bible, we see numerous instances of celebration after victorious battles. The Israelites sang and danced after crossing the Red Sea. David danced with all his might when the Ark of the Covenant returned to Jerusalem. These acts of celebration were not empty rituals; they were powerful acknowledgments of God's faithfulness and the defeat of their enemies.

The Midnight Triumph Ceremony

To celebrate your victories in the midnight warfare, consider creating a "Midnight Triumph Ceremony." This is a sacred time set apart to reflect, praise, and give thanks for all that God has accomplished through you in the spiritual realm.

1. Reflect on Your Journey

Begin by taking a moment to reflect on your journey. Think back to the battles you've faced, the challenges you've overcome, and the breakthroughs you've experienced. Remember the specific prayers and decrees that brought about those victories. This reflection will remind you of God's faithfulness and the progress you've made.

2. Praise and Worship

Now, enter into a time of heartfelt praise and worship. Play worship music that stirs your spirit, and let your heart overflow with gratitude. Sing, dance, and raise your hands in worship. Invite the presence of the Holy Spirit to fill the space and join in your celebration.

3. Testimonies and Declarations

Invite fellow midnight warriors to share their testimonies. Encourage them to recount how God has intervened in their lives through midnight prayers and warfare. These testimonies serve as powerful reminders of God's faithfulness and inspire others to continue the battle.

4. Thanksgiving Offerings

Consider offering a thanksgiving offering as an act of faith. Just as the Israelites brought offerings to God after their victories, you can give to your local church or a charitable cause that aligns with your spiritual values. This act of generosity demonstrates your trust in God's provision and your desire to bless others.

5. Communion

Partake in communion as a symbol of your unity with Christ. Remember that the victory you celebrate is ultimately rooted in the finished work of Jesus on the cross. As you partake in the bread and wine (or grape juice), reflect on the price He paid for your freedom.

6. Prophetic Declarations

Release prophetic declarations for the future. Proclaim that your midnight victories are just the beginning, and greater breakthroughs are on the horizon. Use the authority you've gained through your warfare to decree blessings over your life, your family, and your community.

7. Fellowship and Community

Finally, celebrate with fellow believers. Share a meal together, engage in fellowship, and strengthen the bonds of your spiritual community. The unity among warriors is a powerful force that can withstand any attack from the enemy.

Continuing the Journey

As you celebrate your midnight triumph, remember that this is not the end of your journey but a significant milestone. Your victories are evidence of God's power at work in and through you. Use this celebration as a launching pad for future battles and continue to grow in your faith, prayer life, and spiritual authority.

The Midnight Triumph Ceremony is a sacred and powerful practice that reinforces your identity as a victorious warrior in Christ. It honors God, encourages your fellow warriors, and propels you forward in your spiritual journey. So, with hearts full of gratitude and faith, celebrate your victories, for they are a testament to the greatness of your God and the effectiveness of your midnight warfare.

Warfare Prayer

1. In the mighty name of Jesus, I declare that I am a victorious warrior, and I celebrate every triumph I've experienced through midnight warfare.

2. I decree that my celebration magnifies the glory of God and increases the impact of my prayers.

3. By the power of the Holy Spirit, I reflect on my journey and remember the battles I've won, giving thanks for God's faithfulness.

4. Lord, I lift my hands in praise and worship, declaring that You are the source of my strength and victory.

5. I declare that the enemy is defeated, and I dance with joy, just as David danced before the Ark of the Covenant.

6. By the authority of Jesus' name, I rebuke any spirit of weariness or discouragement that may try to overshadow my celebration.

7. I release a shout of triumph, for the Lord has gone before me and granted me victory in every battle.

8. I testify of the goodness of God and His mighty works in my life, inspiring others to trust in Him for their breakthroughs.

9. I offer a thanksgiving offering, believing that my giving will open doors of blessings and provision in my life.

10. As I partake in communion, I declare that I am one with Christ, and His victory is my victory.

11. I decree that the finished work of Jesus on the cross secures my triumph in every spiritual battle.

12. In the name of Jesus, I prophesy greater breakthroughs and victories in the future, for I am an overcomer.

13. I declare that the power of the enemy is broken over my life and my loved ones.

14. By the blood of Jesus, I cancel every assignment of darkness that seeks to hinder my celebration.

15. I release healing and restoration in Jesus' name, declaring that I walk in divine health and wholeness.

16. I decree that fear and doubt have no place in my heart, for I am filled with the peace and confidence of Christ.

17. I declare that I am a watchman in the midnight hour, alert and vigilant against the schemes of the enemy.

18. By the authority of Jesus, I dismantle strongholds and cast down every high thing that exalts itself against the knowledge of God.

19. I proclaim that I am a child of light, and darkness cannot comprehend or overpower the light within me.

20. I release a mantle of discernment, that I may see through deception and walk in truth.

21. I declare that I am empowered by the Holy Spirit to pray with boldness and authority.

22. I rebuke the spirit of complacency and declare that I am on fire for God, zealous in my pursuit of Him.

23. In the name of Jesus, I invoke the presence of angels to encamp around me and protect me from all harm.

24. I declare that my worship is a sweet fragrance to God, and it ushers me into His presence.

25. I release supernatural dreams and visions, that I may receive divine revelations and guidance.

26. By the bloodline covenant, I secure my family and loved ones, declaring that they are covered by the blood of Jesus.

27. I proclaim that every prayer I utter is a powerful weapon that shatters the plans of the enemy.

28. I am fearless and courageous, for I know that God is with me, and no weapon formed against me shall prosper.

29. I declare that I walk in victory, and the chains of bondage are broken in every area of my life.

30. I release a spirit of revival, that the fire of God may spread throughout my community and nation.

31. I declare that I am a history maker, and my midnight triumphs leave a legacy of faith for future generations.

32. By the authority of Jesus, I release miracles, signs, and wonders in my life and the lives of those I pray for.

33. I declare that I am a vessel of honor, sanctified and set apart for the Lord's service.

34. I rebuke every hindrance to my destiny and declare that I walk in the divine purpose God has ordained for me.

35. I proclaim that I am a conqueror, and no power of darkness can stand against the name of Jesus.

36. I release the anointing of the Holy Spirit to break every yoke of bondage in my life and the lives of others.

37. I declare that I am an ambassador of Christ, representing His kingdom with authority and grace.

38. By the power of the blood of Jesus, I cleanse my mind, soul, and spirit from all defilement.

39. I decree that I am an overcomer by the blood of the Lamb and the word of my testimony.

40. In Jesus' name, I seal these declarations and celebrate my victories with unwavering faith, knowing that the battle is the Lord's, and I am more than a conqueror through Him who loves me. Amen.

Appreciation

Thank you for purchasing and reading my book. I am extremely grateful and hope you found value in reading it. Please consider sharing it with friends and family and leaving a review online.

Your feedback and support are always appreciated and allow me to continue doing what I love.

Please go to www.amazon.com
if you'd like to leave a review.

Deliverance & Spiritual Warfare

- Monitoring spirits exposed and defeated
- Jezebel spirit exposed and defeated
- Marine spirits exposed and defeated
- Prophetic warfare: Unleashing supernatural power in warfare
- Rise above the curse: An empowering guide to overcome witchcraft attacks
- The time is now: A guide to overcoming marital delay
- Earth moving prayers: Pray until miracles happen
- I must win this battle: Expanded edition
- I must my financial battle
- Essential prayers
- Open heavens: Unlocking divine blessings and breakthroughs
- This battle ends now
- Breaking the unbreakable
- Reversing evil handwriting
- I must win this battle - French edition
- I must win this battle - Spanish edition
- Ammunition for spiritual warfare
- Reversing the Irreversible
- Let there be a change
- Total Deliverance: Volume 1
- 21 days prayer for total breakthroughs

- Warrior Mom: Defending your children in the court of heaven.
- Breaking Chains of Rejection: A personal deliverance manual
- Overcoming afflictions in the workplace
- The art of spiritual vision casting
- Thriving beyond letdowns: Overcoming constant disappointments
- Breaking the Family Curse: Unraveling the Past for a Brighter Future and Transform Your Family Legacy
- The Anointed Intercessor: A Prayer Warrior's Calling
- Prayers of the Midnight Warriors

Weapons of Warfare
- The Name of Jesus: The unstoppable weapon of warfare
- Praise and Worship: Potent weapons of warfare
- Blood of Jesus: The ultimate weapon
- The Word of God as a weapon: A double-edged sword to bring transformation and unparallel victory in spiritual warfare.
- Praying with Power: The warrior's guide to weapon of dynamic warfare prayer
- The weapon of prophetic dreams
- Praying in tongues of heaven
- Waging war through fasting: The incontestable weapon of spiritual warfare
- The fire of God's presence: A weapon of unparallel strength & potency
- The Word of Testimony – A stealth weapon of spiritual warfare
- Angelic Assistance in Spiritual Warfare

Power of Anointing

- The power of anointing for success: Partnering with God in extraordinary moments for great success
- The Power of Anointing for Generational Wealth

14 Days Prayer & Fasting Series

- 14 Days prayer to break evil patterns.
- 14 days prayer against delay and stagnation
- 14 days prayer for a new beginning
- 14 days prayer for deliverance from demonic attacks
- 14 days prayer for total healing
- 14 days prayer for deliverance from rejection and hatred
- 14 days prayer for healing the foundations
- 14 days prayer for breaking curses and evil covenants
- 14 days prayer for uncommon miracles
- 14 days prayer for restoration and total recovery
- 14 days prayer: It's time for a change
- 14 days prayer for deliverance from witchcraft attacks
- 14 days prayer for accelerated promotion
- 14 days prayer for deliverance from generational problems
- 14 days prayer for supernatural supply
- 14 days prayer to God's will for your life
- 14 days prayer for Mountaintop Experience
- 14 days prayer for home, family and marriage restoration
- 14 days prayer to overcome stubborn situations.

- 14 days prayer for restoration of stolen destiny
- 14 days prayer for financial breakthroughs

Personal Finances
- The art of utility bills negotiation
- From strapped to successful: Unlocking financial freedom beyond Paycheck to paycheck
- Escape the rat race: How to retire in five years or less.
- Mastering mean reversion: A guide to profitable trading, so simple a 10-year-old can understand

Bible Study
- The King is coming
- Seven judgments of the Bible
- The miracle of Jesus Christ
- The book of Exodus
- Lost and found: The house of Israel
- The parables of Jesus Christ

Fiction
- The merchant's legacy: A tale of faith and family
- A world unraptured: Brink of oblivion
- Gone: A chronicle of chaos

Family Counseling

- Healing whispers: Biblical comfort and healing for men after miscarriage

Leadership/Business
- The most intelligent woman: A woman's guide to outsmarting any room at any level
- Thriving in the unknown: Preparing children for careers that don't exist yet.
- Communication breakthrough: Cultivating deep connections through active listening
- Overcoming Procrastination

Spiritual Growth
- Divine Intimacy: Embracing the Transformative Power of Intimate Communion to Discover Profound Connection and Fulfillment

Theology/Ministry
- Laughing Pulpit: Using humor to enhance preaching.

Parenting/Relationship
- Embracing metamorphosis: Nurturing teenage girls' remarkable journey into adulthood

Marriage/Family

- The conscious husband: Mastering active listening in marriage.
- The conscious wife: Nurturing relationship with awareness, building a perfect and flourishing family.
- Conscious parenting: Mastering active listening to your children.
- From cradle to consciousness: Guiding your child's awareness
- The 'Not Tonight' syndrome: Overcoming false excuses in marital intimacy.

End-Times

- Dawn of eternity: Unraveling the rapture of the saints
- Signs of the end-times: Deciphering prophecies in a race against time
- The rise of the Antichrist: Unveiling the beast and the prophecies

order #
31847570

Total AV
ID 15825 65 38

New P/W V Z 2PTU
NE3crystAl
username
menervacrystel
support@totalav.com

Made in the USA
Monee, IL
06 September 2024

65234996R00184